"Written in a compelling and interesting way, this book is packed full of unique examples and good practises based on new educational paradigms."

Eric Slaats, *Associate Lector, Fontys University ICT - open education, HILL Certified Trainer*

"*Dialogic Feedback for High Impact Learning* is a ground-breaking work that sheds a new light on the use of the most powerful tool in learning and teaching that fits the learning of youngsters of the 21ˢᵗ century. The book reads fluently and shows step-by-step how the learning of both the children and the adults of the future could learn with greater impact. If we care about how professionals will be able to cope with our knowledge-based high technological society of the future, this book should be in the professional toolkit of everyone involved in learning in schools, businesses and universities."

Sari Lindblom, *Professor of Higher Education, Rector of the University of Helsinki, Finland*

Dialogic Feedback for High Impact Learning

In recent years, the transmission paradigm of learning and teaching is making way for new approaches fuelled in part by the technology and AI revolutions. Learning is seen now more often in the light of connectivism, collaboration and creative problem solving. *Dialogic Feedback for High Impact Learning* explores this fascinating trend championing learning as a dialogic process between learners and coaches where learning is connecting networks and resources and leads to creative problem solving. It addresses the need for feedback as a dialogue in training for tomorrow, what it entails and how you can best deal with it.

The book explores the power of feedback in a high-impact learning setting, where all parties strive for a learning and feedback culture rather than a consumption and testing culture. The authors discuss the feedback process, feedback seeking behaviour and the quality of the feedback message, sharing tips for software and apps to support this process and how teachers and coaches from a variety of settings have integrated the feedback dialogue into their training.

This book is intended for everyone who wants to contribute to the learning culture of tomorrow, including learning coaches, managers, education and training professionals, and teachers and trainees at all levels in education.

Filip Dochy is Professor of Learning and Development at the European Academy of Science (Academia Europeae) and a TOP1% scientist at USERN. He is the founder of EAPRIL and past president of EARLI. He is also the founding editor of the journals *Educational Research Review* and *Frontline Learning Research*.

Mien Segers is Professor of Corporate Learning at the Business School at Maastricht University. She is Editor of the EARLI book series 'New perspectives on Learning and Instruction'. In 2021, she received the Belgian Francqui Prize in Brussels as a foreign professor for, among other things, her work on high-impact learning.

Simla Arikan is a postdoctoral researcher from Hacettepe University in Ankara and, since 2019, has been affiliated with the High-Impact Learning Academy. She specialises in effects of visuals on language learning, educational innovation and modes of high-impact learning.

Dialogic Feedback for High Impact Learning

Key to PCP-Coaching and Assessment-as-Learning

FILIP DOCHY, MIEN SEGERS AND SIMLA ARIKAN

Routledge
Taylor & Francis Group

LONDON AND NEW YORK

Cover image: Halyna Shapoval (alika.sun7@gmail.com)

First published 2023
by Routledge
4 Park Square, Milton Park, Abingdon, Oxon OX14 4RN

and by Routledge
605 Third Avenue, New York, NY 10158

Routledge is an imprint of the Taylor & Francis Group, an informa business

British Library Cataloguing-in-Publication Data
A catalogue record for this book is available from the British Library

Library of Congress Cataloging-in-Publication Data
Names: Dochy, F. J. R. C. (Filip J. R. C.), author. | Segers, Mien, author.
| Arikan, Simla, author.
Title: Dialogic feedback for high impact learning : key to PCP-coaching and assessment-as-learning / Filip Dochy, Mien Segers, Simla Arikan.
Description: Abingdon, Oxon ; New York, NY : Routledge, 2023. | Includes bibliographical references and index.
Identifiers: LCCN 2022014412 | ISBN 9781032277967 (hardback) | ISBN 9781032277981 (paperback) | ISBN 9781003294139 (ebook)
Subjects: LCSH: Feedback (Psychology) | Employees--Coaching of. | Employees--Training of. | Communication in personnel management. | Learning.
Classification: LCC BF319.5.F4 D64 2023 | DDC 153.6--dc23/eng/20220716
LC record available at https://lccn.loc.gov/2022014412

ISBN: 978-1-032-27796-7 (hbk)
ISBN: 978-1-032-27798-1 (pbk)
ISBN: 978-1-003-29413-9 (ebk)

DOI: 10.4324/9781003294139

Typeset in Dante and Avenir
by KnowledgeWorks Global Ltd.

About Feedback

Feedback is a we-word! **Feedback is the core of Assessment-as-Learning!** We feedback. Feedback gives you wings! Feedback, the banquet for champions! Effective feedback is always dialogue. Feedback is reflecting, chilling and creating depth! **PCP coaching: progress-oriented, content-oriented and process-oriented coaching as a habit.** Feedback is connection, feed-up, feedback and feedforward. Feedback is the core of learning and being able to deal with emotions. Self-efficacy. Connectivism and hybrid expansivism.

Peer feedback. Feedback literacy. E-feedback. Continuous constructive feedback. Feedback with impact is cyclical, frequent, interacting, communicative, specific and understandable, with learner agency, with an action plan, with a follow-up. Feedback seeking/requesting; feedback sharing in interaction/dialogue; understanding feedback; accepting feedback; turning feedback into action. PCP coaching: progress or growth, deepening content and understanding and working optimally in terms of process.

Contents

High-Impact Learning Academy xii

Introduction: Feedback is critical to
'Assessment-as-Learning' and 'Coaching' 1

Part I What do you need to know about feedback? 7

1 Feedback, how did we use to do it? 9

2 Feedback is the core of learning 17

3 Feedback as the core of learning: Central themes 28

4 Feedback-seeking behaviour 42

5 Types of feedback 49

6 The impact of feedback 57

Part II Impactful feedback is dialogue 59

7 Where did the idea of feedback as
dialogue come from? 61

8   Feedback as dialogue, what does it mean?   65

9   Characteristics of a feedback dialogue
    that stimulates learning   71

10 The team feedback dialogue   75

11 Power relationships   78

12 The feedback dialogue in practice   83

13 Barriers to impactful feedback dialogue   86

14 Feedback dialogue as the core of effective
    PCP coaching   90

Part III   Practical examples and tools   97

15 The MoL: MSc learning and development
    in organisations   99

16 The MET learning hubs   104

17 Gilde Training Programmes about well-being   107

18 Avans HR academy   112

19 Fontys ICT open   118

Part IV   Some further tips and answering some
          frequently asked questions   121

20 Feedback dialogues: Where do I get the time?   123

21 How do people experience feedback
    dialogues in practice?   125

22 Professionalisation of teachers with
    respect to feedback   127

23 Software to support feedback dialogues   133

24 Simple feedback tools   148

   Continue with feedback dialogues: How?   151

   References   155

High-Impact Learning Academy

Learning and Development for your future!

→ Innovating your training?
→ Rebuilding your program?
→ Implementing high-impact learning?
→ Training your team in PCP coaching?
→ Using Assessment-as-Learning?
→ Strengthening learner agency? Making your students self-responsible as well?
→ Learning to use feedback dialogues?
→ Designing hybrid learning?
→ Strengthening knowledge assurance?
→ HILL training for your team? Or HILL certification?

Contact our trainers and scientists at: www.highimpactlearningthatlasts.com or mail to Wibran Dochy at info@highimpactlearningthatlasts.com.

Introduction

Feedback is critical to 'Assessment-as-Learning' and 'Coaching'

Feedback is essential for learning. We have known that for a long time. Starting in 1995, there was a strong growth in research and know-how about feedback as a concept or tool. This research thus took place in the period of the growing success of constructivism (the learning theory that assumes that the learner constructs the knowledge himself). However, in everyday practice, there was still a strong dominance of the transmission paradigm, whereby someone at the front of the class teaches or reads slides while the learners try to stay attentive. Then, the learners memorise 'the material' at home and at a usually agreed time they try to reproduce it or perform the skills themselves. In everyday practice at that time, there was little or no mention of high-impact learning or of the theoretical paradigms called 'connectivism' and 'hybrid expansivism'. Connectivism describes learning as a process of connecting networks and information sources. Hybrid expansivism states that learning is 'expansive'; learning means developing new knowledge in a hybrid and collaborative way that assumes learner agency and continuous feedback (see also Dochy, Gijbels, Segers, & Van den Bossche, 2022). Programmes based on High Impact Learning that Lasts (HILL) (see Dochy & Segers, 2018; Dochy et al., 2022) or connectivism and hybrid expansivism in which learners themselves determine which challenges or projects they work on, seek continuous feedback themselves, and participate themselves in demonstrating their competences, were not yet born. Even research from 2020 onwards often implicitly assumes a situation in which an instructor 'teaches' and is the main feedback giver in a unilateral situation. Concepts such as 'learner agency', 'learning partners', 'Assessment-as-Learning', 'challenges' 'learning hubs' and 'learning coaches' are either unknown here or are dead letters.

DOI: 10.4324/9781003294139-1

Yet over the past 30 years, ideas, theories, research and practices about training have changed significantly, especially under the influence of the exponential increase in technology, information accessibility, AI (artificial intelligence), VR (virtual reality), XR (augmented reality) and robotics.

Wasn't it arguably one of the world's most famous business leaders Ricardo Semler, who said 'we are not going to ask our children to memorise everything they can find on Google in two seconds'? Education of young people and adults must therefore be different and we have seen this development unfold before our eyes since 2000.

This book addresses the need for feedback as a dialogue in tomorrow's education. Whereas in the past a multitude of tests and exams took away all sense of learning, led to demotivation, to doing only what had to be done, to a culture of punishment and fear, to examination traumas for a whole section of the population, to a reality of forgetting everything shortly after the test (Harlen & Deakin Crick, 2003), in short to 'low-impact learning', we are now striving for a training model in which the learner, full of interest and urgency, takes up the challenges and learns to assess his own level, performance and competence by means of strong coaching. And just like in traditional training models, the learning coach (also read teacher, trainer, lecturer) is an important figure, with one essential difference: instead of literally and figuratively standing in front of the learners, he stands next to the learners in order to plan, monitor and adjust the learning process together. Here, the feedback dialogue plays a crucial role.

Feedback is at the heart of Assessment-as-Learning. 'Assessment-as-Learning' is one of the building blocks of high-impact learning (Dochy & Segers, 2018; Dochy, Segers, & Dochy, 2020) and can be read as 'the collection and interpretation of meaningful information about the learning process and learning outcomes as an integral part of the learning process'. Assessment-as-Learning with the central role of feedback gets rid of the 'test culture' (Birenbaum, 1996). This culture of testing is referred to by Harland and Wald (2021) as the 'arms race', a metaphor used to explain the phenomenon of the (still increasing) large number of tests.

The metaphor of the 'arms race' was used intentionally because it illustrates a process of assessment proliferation in which, according to this research, teachers have three specific assumptions about learner motivation: (1) learners do not work for something that does not earn a grade, and so teachers do not give assignments that do not have a grade attached to them; (2) in the modular system, learners are given limited choice and teachers constantly compete with each other for learner's time and attention, so grades have to be used as a reward to compete; and (3) learners are complicit in the arms race because they insist on many small tests as a kind of safety net. In such a testing culture (Birenbaum, 1996), every grade counts and even grades on small (so-called formative) tests are seen as 'high stakes' because they all mostly contribute to a final grade (Harland & Wald, 2021).

The benefits of testing for students are well documented. Test results are said to provide information about where the learner stands in the acquisition of intended competences or achievement of goals. They thus provide the opportunity for so-called formative feedback and at the same time are inputs for teachers to identify at-risk students.

To enjoy these benefits, however, giving a grade that counts is superfluous. Learning activities such as assignments, essays and so on, according to Harland and Wald (2021), provide a wealth of information about learning processes and learning outcomes and are thus a much more relevant source than traditional tests (tests, exams) for feedback and the timely identification of students with problems so that they can seek help in time. On top of this, a 'grade-poor' education has many other advantages.

In the case of frequent testing with grades, the learning process of the learner is to a large extent controlled by the testing system: jumping from one hurdle to the next. The tests are the motive for studying (can you call this 'learning'?). There is little or no choice for the learner to steer his learning process, no room to participate in learning activities at his own discretion, needs and/or interests. Therefore, he can hardly exercise agency. The controlling assessment system encourages learners to take study decisions on the basis of often meaningless information such as test or examination scores, to choose modules because they are 'easy' and therefore yield high scores without much effort (even if they are not interested in them), because they yield the required number of credit points and so on. Harland and Wald (2021) aptly summarise this as submission to the demands of the assessment regime.

The arms race or test culture is a didactic approach to control (Wass et al., 2015) that takes away the ability to shape the learning process independently, under one's own responsibility and direction. The constant threat of a summative test is a power game and, according to Harland and Wald (2021), leads to subordination and 'domestication' or 'pampering' of students and creates a culture of dependence with controllable or 'tame' students. In a number-driven system, there is little or no room for depth and essential interaction, self-direction or engagement.

Harland and Wald (2021) express it as follows:

> Lecturers now have total control of student learning and behaviour through a strict diet of summative assessments, whereas constructive scholarly relationships between students and teachers require a

measure of equality, co-operation and agency. The present regime clearly produces compliant students, but in addition to an exercise of repressive power, in a Foucauldian sense, there also seems to be a normalising element at play here. It has been argued that the frequent grading of internal assessments is in the best interest of students and this idea has shaped thinking in both the student and academic staff bodies, both of whom unconsciously accept this culture as a normal and legitimate part of university life. That is, until they are questioned and asked to carefully reflect on such practices.

(p. 113)

Why do educational institutions cling so tightly to the culture of tests and grades? Many educators seriously doubt whether learners will make an effort if there are no grades to be earned. Ecclestone already argued in 1999 that such an instrumental attitude of just doing what is necessary for the tests or just doing what has to be done ensures that learners are no longer prepared to do something challenging or to figure out or solve something cognitively complex. This has everything to do with doubts about 'urgency', 'learner drive', 'learner agency' and whether learners will take responsibility (Ecclestone, 1999).

The many 'high-impact learning' programmes in European countries clearly show a different picture: learners are committed, take responsibility (both 12-year old and 20-year old) and work harder with more pleasure (Dochy et al., 2020). In short, there is an alternative and this alternative works.

Feedback is also the core of coaching. In this book, we call it progress, content and process (PCP) coaching. When coaching learning processes, we will use feedback to coach both content and process (both at team level and individual level), but also to monitor progress and thus ensure an appropriate learning rhythm. Feedback is also a key element in this, both in PCP coaching, in order to achieve learning impact with a strong depth and thus a long-term effect.

This book explores the power of feedback in a high-impact learning culture, where all parties strive for a learning culture and a feedback culture rather than a consumption and testing culture. The need for insights into the power of feedback is evident from the findings of national surveys of, for example, higher education students around the world, regardless of institution or discipline. These show that until recently not only tests or exams, but also feedback practices have consistently received low satisfaction scores (Hill & West, 2020). The solution to this problem is often sought with the learners: they must learn to understand and use the feedback much better.

That is called better feedback literacy (e.g. Carless & Boud, 2018). However, is this really a solution to the problem?

Based on current scientific research, we believe that a solution must go further. The solution lies in in-depth and cyclical feedback dialogues in which the learner has important responsibility ('agency'). In this book, we want to give answers to the 'what' and 'how' questions of the feedback dialogue.

Who is this book for?

This book is intended for everyone who wants to contribute to the learning culture of tomorrow, such as learning coaches, managers, education and training professionals, HRD and education professionals. Those who continue to believe in the eternal value of the paradigm of knowledge transfer with its need for frequent one-sided testing should read another book.

What is the structure of this book?

In the first part, we start with a reflective step: if there is so much knowledge about feedback, why is the practice so stubborn? Then, we will discuss the phenomenon of feedback and the central themes in the scientific literature on feedback. Because learner agency, that is, the learner being in control of his own learning process, is essential for impactful learning, we pay explicit attention to feedback-seeking behaviour. Seeking feedback is an important step in the feedback process. Next, we describe the different types of feedback. If there is so much knowledge about feedback, do we also have evidence about its impact? We list an overview of the most important research results.

In Part II, we connect to an insight that was constantly around the corner in Part I, namely feedback has an impact on learning when it is dialogical. The central topic of Part II is therefore feedback dialogue. We discuss six themes: the origin of the idea of feedback dialogue, the meaning, the characteristics of an impactful feedback dialogue, the role of power and relationships, what does a feedback dialogue look like in practice and what are the conditions for this practice to actually work. Finally, we pay explicit attention to the feedback dialogue as the core of effective PCP coaching.

In Part III, we present five practical examples of how the feedback dialogue is implemented: the master's programme Learning and Development in Organisations, the MET learning hubs, Gilde learning programmes on well-being, Fontys IT open and Avans HR Academy.

In Part IV, we provide some further tips and practical guidelines for feedback dialogues. We emphasise aspects that seemed very important in practice: How do you get enough time for all those feedback dialogues? How do learners experience this in practice? How important is professionalisation of teachers/trainers/coaches with regard to feedback dialogues and how do you set that up? Which software can support feedback dialogues in a meaningful way? And finally: can it be done with simple tools?

What do you need to know about feedback?

1

A fellow professor, Nobel Prize winner in physics, replied to my email asking if he, as a leading scientist, knew where a top talent should study in Europe: 'All the European universities ... that I know anything about are still medieval in their approach to teaching.' And yet we have known for quite a long time that active learning and feedback are the keys to doing things differently.

Actually, each of us has a fairly clear idea about what feedback is. Feedback is usually defined as the communication of information by an external source (sources) about one or more aspect(s) of the learner's (individual or team) functioning and/or his/her completed task or assignment, with the aim of changing (meta)cognition, motivation and/or the learner's behaviour and thus optimising performance(s) (Duijnhouwer, 2010; Gabelica, Van den Bossche, Segers, & Gijselaers, 2012). Already in 2005, we wrote:

> The purpose of feedback is to help the learner recognise his own strengths and weaknesses and thus contribute to the understanding of the steps that the learner will have to take to achieve more professional competence development. Feedback thus acts as advice to improve learning and competence development. In the assessment culture in which support for the learning process is given a leading role, we can state that feedback functions as the engine of the educational learning process. Assessment provides information that should result in development-oriented feedback to the student. In this way, feedback provides the basis of guidance on the road to professionalisation.
>
> (Dochy & Nickmans, 2005, p. 52)

DOI: 10.4324/9781003294139-2

Feedback is a phenomenon that has received much attention in research for decades and is also frequently mentioned in practice. What is striking in many studies and in practice is that even up to 2021, professionals and renowned researchers are writing about feedback as a phenomenon of 'giving', providing and reaching out. Does this fit within the current state of the art of what we know about effective learning?

In this section, we start with a look back: How did we give feedback in the past and why didn't it work? Then, we give a brief introduction to recent learning theories and what they mean for the phenomenon of feedback. Next, we discuss central themes in the feedback literature: methods of giving feedback, quality of the feedback message, the feedback recipient's reaction and the process of feedback.

After that, we elaborate on a theme that has received a lot of attention in the literature on workplace feedback in particular, namely feedback-seeking behaviour.

In the next chapter, we reflect on what the feedback process traditionally looks like or looks like in many training programmes and the question why we do not provide effective feedback.

This is the stepping stone to the question: What do we know about the effects of feedback?

This question brings us to the central topic of this book, namely, impactful feedback is dialogue. The why, what and how of the feedback dialogue is central in Part II.

Feedback, how did we use to do it?   1

Until a few years ago, feedback was almost always one way. The teacher took care of corrections by indicating errors, often on paper, and preferably also giving the right answer. Often, it was just a sheet of paper with red notes or check marks. The learner was not always interested in the feedback. The feedback often had little substantive value, often came far too late and did not attract the attention of the learner who had long been satisfied (or completely discouraged) by the grade received. Very occasionally, the opportunity for oral feedback was offered, but our own experience showed that only a handful of students turned up for such sessions. We received numerous testimonies showing that in all kinds of learning situations, learners simply did not show up at feedback sessions.

Voerman, Meijer, Korthagen and Simons (2012) conducted research into teachers' feedback practices and found not only that little positive feedback was given, but also that explanations were often lacking and that feedback was almost exclusively given after the completion of the learning activities. As might be expected from the above, they also found that learners often did not understand the feedback and/or did not use it.

Until recently, there was a belief that learners were not particularly interested in feedback and did not want to put in the effort. A study by Blair and McGinty (2013) took a different view. Students made rather strong statements, such as

> Oh my experience ... I feel like I have to run after it. If I want feedback, I have to try and pull it out of the lecturers and that means chasing them by email, knocking on their door during office hours, or knocking on their door outside of office hours. Chasing them after

DOI: 10.4324/9781003294139-3

lectures, before lectures, before the seminar, after the half-hour, during the seminar ... And then, it's ok, it's kind of like they're in a hurry to get rid of me – maybe – and they say 'yeah yeah yeah generally fine', all that kind of stuff and then at the end, when I get my essay back it's not the grade I expected for all that running around, you know. So I would say their advice wasn't that great, they didn't really pay attention when they gave it to me.

and

I found that I had to look for feedback if I wanted to; nobody gave you feedback voluntarily. If you went and asked, you could get some more detailed feedback, but you really had to agree to see people during their office hours and ask them very detailed questions.

(Blair & McGinty, 2013, p. 474)

The metaphors students used, 'running after feedback', 'chasing teachers' and 'chasing', indicate how difficult obtaining oral feedback had been in many courses up to that point. It can hardly be said that students make no attempt to obtain feedback or do anything with it.

We are happy with all the recent changes in this respect, but actually one can say that 'traditional education' made it structurally impossible for feedback to have any impact. Conditions for realising impact are trust, no link to grades, feedback is cyclical and the feedback giver is accessible. By dividing content into all kinds of subjects and modules that are offered by different instructors, little trust is established; there is no time for extensive feedback and so only brief feedback is given after a test or score; since the component is then completed, there is also no follow-up on the feedback; and as the research above shows, instructors (who occasionally teach for an hour) are difficult or impossible to reach. These are some of the elements (you will find more in this book) that ensure that this cocktail can never lead to impact.

Many researchers have been pointing in a different direction for years: new assessment culture, more feedback, no more fear culture, no more tests and exams that lead to demotivation and quick forgetting, more interaction and more trust, etc. (Dochy, Segers, et al., 2003). Black and McCormick (2010), for example, argued that in higher education there should be more attention to verbal than written feedback, that more explanation is needed about strategies to increase autonomy in learning and that more harmony is needed between assessment moments with a formative and summative purpose.

The assessment culture (development culture) was announced by Birenbaum and Dochy (1996) as a science-based alternative to the test culture (judgment culture). Cartney (2010) and Nicol (2010) later announced, along with many others, that the new assessment culture was emerging, which included the use of self and peer assessment to promote student self-regulation. Yet the evolution did not go as fast as it was expected and desired. The gap between old and new was stubborn, including the gap around feedback.

Why don't students learn from 'normal' feedback?

The reason for this appears to be the famous 'feedback gap'. Various researchers wrote about 'Exploring the Feedback Gap', in which 'Student Inability to Benefit from Feedback' was sometimes mentioned in the same breath. In our opinion, 'Trainer's/teacher's inability to pass feedback' could also be mentioned. Both are probably equally important.

Hill and West (2020) report that, in addition to testing, feedback consistently leads to dissatisfaction among students all over the world: 'Perhaps because of these numerous difficulties, assessment and feedback receive consistently low satisfaction scores in national student surveys of higher education around the world, irrespective of institution or discipline' (p. 83). According to Evans (2013), student and also teacher dissatisfaction with feedback is frequently reported and is known as the 'feedback gap': on the one hand, learners complain most about technical aspects of feedback, such as content, organisation of assessment activities, timing and lack of clarity about requirements (Higgins, Hartley, & Skelton, 2001; Huxham, 2007); on the other hand, teachers complain that students do not make use of feedback or do not take action in response to feedback.

Some authors refer to a kind of inability of learners to take advantage of feedback opportunities (Bloxham & Campbell, 2010; Fisher, Cavanagh, & Bowles, 2011). Even with good quality feedback, the gap continues to play a blocking role. According to Taras (2003),

> this has to do with the complexity of how students understand, use and give feedback. Feedback is not a piece of stand-alone information, it requires the feedback giver to understand what exactly underlies a good performance or process or the mistakes that were made. In short, feedback is part of a learning process in which all those involved are active. The understanding and use of feedback can only

be effective when there is a dialogue between all those involved so that misinterpretations can be avoided and/or resolved.

Young (2000) also refers to the complexity of the feedback process as an explanation for the feedback gap. Individual variables influence the perception and use of feedback (Young, 2000), specific learning contexts are often complex and not all learners and coaches are equally competent in giving and receiving feedback.

The lack of a learning effect is also an important area of research. Many of these studies, however, depart from an outdated paradigm in which the expert provides corrective feedback so that the learner can give exactly the answer the instructor expects. This is no longer the case, according to gurus such as Ricardo Semler, Juval Harari and many others.

Within that 'transfer paradigm', Weaver (2006) points out the role of the level of intellectual maturity. Fritz and Morris (2000) argued that prior knowledge plays a major role in learners' perceptions and responses, and that misconceptions are highly resistant to correction. Cognitive abilities play a role in how individuals understand information (Liu & Carless, 2006) and emotions also have an impact on how feedback is received and what consequences it has (Värlander, 2008). Well-known emotional dimensions of feedback include the importance of positive feedback for learners' confidence and motivation and the role of expectations of success. If learners have low expectations of success and the tasks seem difficult, they have little motivation to go through and use the feedback information (Wingate, 2010). The expectations of success are determined by the self-efficacy of the learners (Van Dinther, Dochy, & Segers, 2011). Hattie and Timperley (2007) also confirmed that both the level at which feedback is given and the degree of self-efficacy of the learners influence the way in which they subsequently deal with the feedback.

In addition, for a long time, feedback was almost exclusively written and too much one directional, which meant that the effect was very meagre. We will also pay attention to this further on in this book.

Despite all the arguments why feedback often has no effect, it has long been clear in what direction to look for a solution. As early as 1995, Butler and Winne concluded that 'the most effective students generate … internal feedback by testing their performance against self-generated or given criteria' (p. 24) and Handley and Cox (2007) added that they also seek feedback from external sources. So that is the route to take for learners: the starting point of the learner agency in the feedback process is the learner's feedback question which is the beginning of the feedback dialogue. We will come back to this in detail later.

Why don't we give effective feedback?

Many colleagues with whom we have worked for many years or have had academic discussions have done research on how to achieve more effective feedback. We are certainly thinking here of the work of David Carless, Dylan Wiliam, Paul Black, Menucha Birenbaum, John Hattie, Ernesto Panadero and others. Although their work has led to interesting insights such as the importance of evaluation with formative aims (instead of only summative) and the role of feedback literacy among learners, much of this research has been conducted within a framework of outdated paradigms in which learning often takes place in a culture of dependency (teacher-driven instead of student-driven), control and distrust by the teacher with fear on the part of the student, focus on exams by both teachers and students, extrinsically motivated students (getting a passing grade as the primary motive for learning) and curricula predetermined by the programme. However, the aforementioned scholars have already hinted that a learning situation in which there is no trust and no learner agency creates few opportunities for effective feedback.

In test-driven programmes, students show a strong preference for corrective feedback (O'Donovan, Rust, & Price, 2016): just tell me what I need to do to raise my grade. Within this same paradigm, it is therefore not surprising that the discourse is mainly about the student as a consumer, as this paradigm reinforces an instrumental attitude towards learning and prevents students from taking responsibility for their own development (Carless & Boud, 2018). Carless and Boud (2018) highlight that this can lead to students' passive attitude towards feedback and the expectation that it is the teacher's role to tell students what to do to achieve high marks. In such an environment, students feel neither able nor encouraged to decode feedback or take action.

As a solution to the effectiveness problem of feedback, the concept of 'feedback literacy' has gained attention. According to Sutton (2012), feedback literacy would require learners to acquire an academic language necessary to understand, interpret and think with complex ideas. What is important is that learners understand both the purpose and content of feedback, want to receive feedback, can deal with the emotions that feedback evokes and, above all, can name follow-up steps that they plan after the feedback (Dawson et al., 2019). Learners often give defensive responses to feedback, especially in situations where comments are critical or low grades are given. Feedback then leads to negative emotional reactions and can be felt as an attack on the person. Being able to deal with emotional balance will therefore also determine how strong the commitment is to feedback. In order to avoid these ineffective practices and thus develop feedback literacy, it is necessary to use feedback as an intermediary tool (i.e. just do it!), that is (preferably several times), during a learning process (read: having to seek/receive/give feedback continuously on a frequent basis) (Winstone & Carless, 2019).

How then can we achieve an impactful feedback process? Believing that this can be done by, for example, organising a training or course in feedback literacy would be rather naive. It has previously been shown that setting up the feedback process as a continuous dialogue can be an effective method to this end. We found clear indications of this in the work of Carless and Boud (2018) who indicate that the personalised and more engaging approach in audio feedback is valued by learners and leads to high engagement.

Ajjawi and Boud (2018) explicitly emphasise the shaping of an effective feedback dialogue between learner and learning coach. For example, research showed that affective-emotional responses to feedback are mediated by students' relationships with their teacher and peers, as together they construct meaning about where the learning process is going and where it is faltering, why this is so, what feedback demand is and what follow-up steps are needed (Esterhazy & Damsa, 2017).

Using feedback in the learning process as a dialogue between all those involved has consequences for all aspects of the learning environment (Carless & Boud, 2018). If feedback is a dialogue between all those involved with the learner's feedback question as the starting point, this only works when throughout the learning process the learner has a high degree of responsibility in his learning process or is in charge of his learning process, that is, when a core building block of the learning environment is learner agency. The concept of feedback as dialogue fits within a learning environment where collaborative learning and joint knowledge development have an important place, where learning processes start from the learner's question, interest and need (urgency). In short, a feedback dialogue is a 'natural' aspect of a HILL (High Impact Learning that Lasts) learning environment (Dochy, Segers, & Dochy, 2020).

What are the conditions for an impactful feedback dialogue? Of course, the characteristics of quality feedback that we summarise further in Box 3.1 also apply. From the perspective of feedback as a dialogue, we add here a number of conditions that are often mentioned by authors about the process of giving feedback. First of all, a feedback dialogue stimulates the learning process when it challenges the learner to consider and discuss new approaches and perspectives with the other partners in the dialogue. Daring to take on challenges requires the learner to have a high degree of self-efficacy, intrinsic motivation and the ability to deal with emotions (success and failure). In addition, an impactful feedback dialogue requires qualitative interaction and communication: the nature and tone during the feedback dialogue also determine whether learners accept the feedback and take action (Lipnevich, Berg, & Smith, 2016). When the respect and commitment of all those involved in the feedback dialogue is clear, the commitment to take further action with the feedback increases. Incidentally, only in a culture of trust will all those involved in the feedback dialogue be open to discussing what they do not understand, where there are misinterpretations, what mistakes were made and what they can learn from them (Carless, 2013). Next, just as in a process of giving feedback, the timing of the feedback dialogue plays an important role. A feedback dialogue after a test or an examination does not encourage students to do anything with the feedback, let alone collect or look at it. The grade is usually already fixed and the course unit closed (especially in modular programmes!), and there is no perspective or explicit and concrete possibilities to do something with the new insights based on the feedback dialogue (Carless et al., 2011). One-off feedback dialogues, isolated from the learning process, work at least 'sub-optimally'. Feedback dialogues stimulate the learning process when they are frequent, as is often said 'on-time on-task' (Evans, 2013).

In addition, the coach plays an important role. The coach demystifies the assessment process by using examples, modelling aspects of good practice, clarifying assessment criteria and giving clear signals about good practice (Evans, 2013).

Finally, organising and conducting an effective feedback process requires training as an integral part of professionalisation for coaches and teachers (Evans, 2013).

An overview can be found in Box 1.1.

BOX 1.1

Summary

Why don't we give effective feedback?

- A learning situation where there is no trust and no 'learner agency' creates few opportunities for effective feedback.
- In test-driven training, an instrumental attitude towards learning is increasingly reinforced. This prevents the learner from taking responsibility for their own development and leads to a passive attitude towards feedback.

(Continued)

- When coaches do not indicate in behaviour and language that they care about the learner, the commitment to take further action with the feedback does not increase. Only in a culture of trust do learners admit what they don't understand and what mistakes they made.
- Feedback after a test or exam is not an incentive to do anything with that feedback, let alone retrieve or review the feedback.

How then?

- Central to the feedback dialogue is where one wants to go; the conversation challenges the learner to consider and discuss new approaches and perspectives.
- A feedback dialogue is not only a cognitive process, it also evokes emotions. Being able to deal with this and make it discussable is partly determined by the commitment of all those involved. Organising feedback as a dialogue with a safe, trusting relationship between all involved helps in dealing with emotional reactions to feedback.
- A feedback dialogue offers the possibility to clarify a feedback question, to check if one understands the other and to look together for underlying questions and possible next steps.
- A feedback dialogue has an impact when there is mutual trust and safety, respect and commitment of all those involved in the dialogue.
- Feedback dialogue is an integral part of the learning process, so 'on-time and on-task'.
- Training of coaches to organise and guide feedback dialogues is a necessary part of a professionalisation process.

Feedback is the core of learning

2

It took us almost 20 years to be able to give really good presentations. However, scientists rarely or never give each other feedback on presentations at conferences, for example. Nevertheless, there are always complaints about the pitifully low level of most presentations. An excellent presentation is made by practising and then hearing suggestions for improvement from friends and colleagues: speaking clearly, not always standing in the same place, not so monotonous, giving examples, not reading your slides verbatim, turning them into a story, telling an anecdote, summarising and so on.

The fact that feedback is actually the engine of learning is nothing new (Dochy & Nickmans, 2005). Already in the work of Martens and Dochy (1997), it appeared that feedback has a great influence on the way learners learn and on their engagement. Also, Black and William (1998) emphasised a little later that feedback has a positive effect on learning compared to other interventions.

The term 'feedback' in its current sense was first used, according to Wiliam (2018), by Karl Ferdinand Braun, the winner (along with Guglielmo Marconi) of the 1909 Nobel Prize in Physics.

An example of a positive feedback loop is a recession like the COVID-19 period, in which people lose their jobs or work fewer hours, so they have less money, and thus spend less, which leads to even more job losses, which leads to even more loss of confidence, according to Wiliam (2018). It is positive feedback because the information provided (there is a recession and limit contacts) pushes the system further in the direction it was already going (less economic activity). The effect of the room thermostat is a well-known example of negative feedback: when it gets colder, the system gives feedback and the room is heated again.

DOI: 10.4324/9781003294139-4

Robert Gagné, an American educational psychologist, was the first to emphasise that questions about the quality, accuracy, and frequency of feedback, and how it affected performance, were necessary research questions to unlock the essence of 'learning' (Gagné, 1954). Within the prevailing view of learning and instruction and the role of student and teacher within it, feedback was then seen as unidirectional, corrective within an instructional situation directed and controlled by the teacher. Illustrative is the definition of feedback by Kulhavy: 'any of the numerous procedures that are used to tell a learner if an instructional response is right or wrong' (Kulhavy, 1977, p. 211; see also Wiliam, 2018). Although theorising about learning and instruction and the role of feedback has since evolved in important ways, feedback practice is quasi unchanged. O'Donovan, Rust and Price (2016) refer to this discrepancy between theory and practice as 'the feedback dilemma'. The literature clearly shows that feedback is potentially the most powerful component when it comes to optimising learning (O'Donovan et al., 2016). However, some research also shows that much feedback in practice does not live up to this potential. In practice, feedback still often reflects the ideas of learning theories such as behaviourism and cognitivism.

What do recent learning theories imply for feedback practice?

It is a fundamental principle of the social constructivist process model that knowledge is formed and evolves through increasing participation and that dialogue is a core element of that participation. Activities such as peer discussions supported by coaches engage students in dialogue with each other and the coaches, thereby encouraging and facilitating the learner to develop self-evaluation skills and self-regulation strategies (Carless, Salter, Yang, & Lam, 2011). Handley, Price and Millar (2008) and many others also emphasise the value of dialogue. They point out the crucial importance of trust and psychological safety in ensuring learners' involvement in the feedback process.

Connectivism

The social software that emerged at the beginning of this century added an extra dimension to social constructivism and gave rise to a connectivist view of learning. These social tools have essentially become the space, not the channel, for sense-making (Dochy, Gijbels, Segers, & Van den Bossche, 2022). The value of the networks formed is greater than the value of the specific information and knowledge that flows through a network at a given moment.

Siemens (2005) describes the principles of connectivism, as follows (Dochy et al., 2022):

- Learning and knowledge reside in the diversity of opinions.
- Learning is a process of connecting specialised nodes or sources of information.
- Learning may reside in non-human devices.
- The ability to learn is of greater critical importance than what is currently known.
- Nurturing and maintaining connections are necessary to facilitate continuous learning.
- The ability to see connections between areas, ideas and concepts is a core skill.
- Accurate, up-to-date knowledge is the goal of all connectivist-learning activities.
- Decision-making is a learning process in itself.

Connectivism defines learning as a network phenomenon. It states that learning begins when the learner participates in a learning community where, through the clustering of similar interests, participants interact, share, dialogue and think together (Siemens, 2005). In this context, building on Downes' theory of distributed knowledge (2005), knowledge and learning skills are seen as distributive. This means that networks of connections are built through experience and interactions in learning communities or 'communities of learning'. In the Web 2.0 era, these interactions are not limited to words but can also be represented in images such as video and multimedia. Learning communities are referred to as nodes or knots and can be organisations, libraries, websites, journals, databases or other information sources (Siemens, 2005). Each node is part of a larger network and these networks consist of two or more nodes. It is within these networks that knowledge resides and changes and evolves by flowing in these networks (Dochy et al., 2022).

Connectivism means that learning is a matter of interaction in networks and thus of continuous dialogue and feedback.

Hybrid expansivism

In recent years, based on connectivism, new perspectives have emerged that build on Engeström's theory of expansive learning (see also Dochy, Engeström, Sannino, & Van Meeuwen, 2021) and various innovations in practice, such as the Lumiar approach based on the books of the world-famous business manager Ricardo Semler (Semler, 1993, 2003). Engeström emphasised the importance of creating new knowledge in an era where developments and changes follow each other at an exponential rate. In addition, Semler's philosophy and his enormous economic successes were based on the idea of a high degree of freedom for employees, as long as they perform well. He strongly emphasised the 'agency' of employees or learners and also applied this in his Lumiar schools (https://lumiar.co/en/). Such new approaches reflect what we call 'hybrid expansivism', a perspective with the following main characteristics of learning for the future:

- Learning is expansive: learning to create new knowledge is important.
- The learner's agency is the key to learning.
- Learning is hybrid: an alternation between digital and face-to-face learning.
- A certain balance between formal (structured) learning and informal learning (a wide range of more unstructured ways of learning, supported by technology and reinforced by social networks).
- A balance between the acquisition of basic knowledge and generic competences.
- Learning is collaborative and largely self-directed.
- Learning is based on continuous feedback dialogue (Assessment-as-Learning).

Building further on connectivism, hybrid expansivism is a vision of learning in which continuous feedback dialogue is central to the development of new knowledge in a flexible, collaborative and hybrid learning environment.

In line with hybrid expansivism, we describe feedback as all the interactive exchanges that take place within and outside the immediate learning context, in which information about process and/or performance is requested, given and received, and in which different parties are actively involved (the learner, coach, peers and external parties). We support the view of Ferguson (2011) who states that feedback is a crucial way to help learners develop so that they are able to monitor, assess and regulate their own learning as expected in professional practice (Ferguson, 2011).

Feedback and Assessment-as-Learning

Feedback is often mentioned in the same breath as assessment. In particular, the approach to assessment in which assessment is seen as an integral part of the learning process, feedback occupies a central position. The High

Impact Learning that Last (HILL) model, which was introduced in 2016 and further developed in 2018 and 2020, positions Assessment-as-Learning within the set of building blocks that together ensure an impactful learning process (see Figure 2.1). To quickly introduce the HILL model to managers and learning coaches, we provide a brief overview of the various building blocks, each in a single sentence. This of course means that much nuance and detail is lost, but it gives a rough idea of what learning will look like in the future.

The idea of Assessment-as-Learning is now well established in academic research.

Assessment-as-Learning is mostly defined as integrating learning and assessment.

Assessment-as-Learning is a way of assessing learners that is different from traditional assessment. It is used in order to prevent learners from having fear, from losing their intrinsic motivation and their interest.

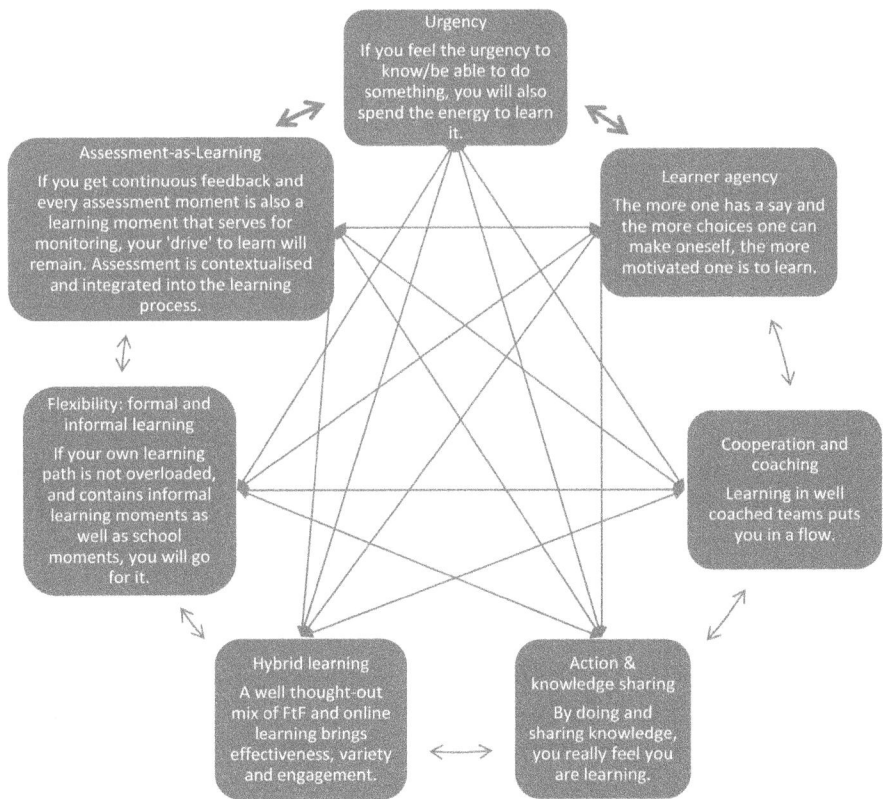

Figure 2.1 The High-Impact Learning that Lasts model (HILL) summarised.

'Assessment-as-Learning' is aiming at being more suited to the modern times of IT and internet, at being more in line with current ways of learning, at being more reliable and providing retention of knowledge and skills on the long term and not just solely at a single testing moment. Assessment-as-Learning involves teachers and learners taking both responsibility for the learning and students playing an active role and that assessment is integrated in the learning process. 'Assessment-as-Learning' occurs when learners monitor their own learning (based on criteria), ask questions and use a range of strategies to decide what they know and can do, and how to use assessment information for new learning.

Dylan Wiliam wrote as early as 2011: '... there is now a strong body of theoretical and empirical work that suggests that integrating assessment with instruction may well have unprecedented power to increase student engagement and to improve learning outcome' (Wiliam, 2011, p. 13). After 10 years, all we can say is that the evidence Wiliam refers to has greatly increased. Nobody doubts anymore that forcing learners by presenting a long test battery is not only demotivating but also has little impact on learning in the long term (for an overview, see Dochy & Segers, 2018). As Wiliam points out, it is an integration of learning and assessment or 'Assessment-as-Learning' that generates an unseen power that leads to learner engagement and an improvement in learning outcomes.

Assessment-as-learning has been increasingly developed as an approach to assessment in recent years on the basis of the so-called 3G assessment.

3G assessment in line with 3G learning theory

The first generation of learning theories (behaviourism) focused strongly on knowledge and reproduction; the second generation (constructivism) had a strong focus on the 'self-construction' of that knowledge base. From the theoretical standpoint of the third generation (3G; social-cultural theory / activity theory, connectivism), access to and use of appropriate tools is the key to 'expansive learning'. Knowledge is created in interaction with others and being able to exercise 'learner agency' (taking the wheel yourself) is central. Tasks are authentic and collaborative in nature where learners are involved in generating problems and solutions, says James (2012). It is important to support these (team) activities in such a way that the learner can carry them out while being coached by others. The learning coach is the 'more expert other', sometimes a teacher but also a peer. It serves as a lever to achieve learning behaviour. Learners and learning coaches solve problems together and develop their competences in order to achieve learning outcomes. However, it is only recently that assessment is being framed within 'activity theory' and goes beyond 'Assessment for Learning'.

So what does 3G assessment mean? As James points out, learning happens through active participation in an authentic (real-world) project. So what does '3G assessment' look like? James describes it as follows: 'The focus here is on how well people exercise "agency" in their use of the resources or tools (intellectual, human, material) available to them to formulate problems, work productively and evaluate their efforts. Learning outcomes can be captured and reported through various forms of recording, including audio and visual media' (James, 2006, p. 58). The exercise of agency also becomes central: Does the student demonstrate an ability to manage the resources and tools in the problem-solving process? Information which cannot be read off from test results at all, but which requires process information. And here she gets to the core of the Assessment-as-Learning approach.

Within this framework, portfolios can be interesting tools, especially when the core of the learning process is to construct a learning identity. Then it is precisely important to make self-assessment central. This is strongly supported by the well-known research of Hattie and Timperley (2007). They found that only one element had a very strong impact, with an effect size of more than 1.4, namely the use of 'self-report' grades or rather the 'expectations' that people have, as they call it. If students' expectations fit with the approach of the programme and the coaching they experience, it leads students to exceeding their own expectations. That, according to Hattie and Timperley, is the only real factor with impact!

In summary, assessment with a more holistic and qualitative character leans towards the goal of Assessment-as-Learning. James (2012) provides some examples of schools using 3G assessment (third generation). From these examples and papers on 3G assessment, we learn that Assessment-as-Learning should be further developed in the following future critical directions (Dochy, Dochy, & Janssens, 2018):

- Authentic assessment based on ongoing performance or 'exit' exhibitions (presentations/exhibitions at the end of a learning period showing what has been learned) is promoted.
- Learners are asked to work in a multidisciplinary way by creating 'real' learning and assessment activities (learner as worker).
- Learners and learning coaches can both present a problem task, as long as they understand the underlying principles that give rise to the problem. Providing learners with an understanding of the meta-level of the problem adds much value to the learning process.
- If learning is contextualised, so must assessment be.

- Assessment integrated into the learning process implies that it is also carried out by the community, rather than just by external assessors. The team thus becomes co-responsible.
- Assessment of team learning is as important as the learning of the individual.
- 'In vivo' studies or 'complex problem solving' are often the appropriate form of assessment.
- Agency should be the central concept in assessing whether and how personal resources, other resources or tools (whether intellectual, human or material) are used to formulate problems, work productively and evaluate efforts. This means, for example, that when students carry out a project together, we discuss afterwards whether they were able to use all the available resources in a qualitative way, the way they used them and so on (i.e. whether they did good 'management') (i.e. whether they have had good 'management').
- Learners are challenged to practice and actively apply the acquired knowledge in new situations.
- Learners improve their ability to effectively convey information orally, graphically and in writing.
- Learners are expected to be reflective, persistent and well organised.
- A focus on learning is described on the basis of the goals set by the learner. These learning objectives can be adapted during the learning process; they are not fixed or strictly defined.

Mary James mentioned a couple of examples of Assessment-as-Learning she found back in 2012. One came from 'The Coalition of Essential Schools' (CES) founded by Theodore Sizer in the USA. They use a model of authentic assessment based on continuous presentations or 'exit exhibitions' in which learning in different disciplines can be demonstrated and evaluated. Such 'exit exhibitions' have the following characteristics:

- It asks students to work cross-curricularly in a respectful way by creating 'real' learning activities. The dominant metaphor is 'student-as-worker'.
- Tasks are not necessarily devised by teachers; students can devise them themselves, provided they understand the principles underlying their construction. Helping students to acquire this meta-level understanding is a valued pedagogical objective.
- It asks students to practice using accumulated knowledge and applying it to new situations.
- It insists on effective communication in a number of forms of expression: oral, written and graphic.

- It requires students to be reflective, persistent and well organised.
- It creates a focus for learning by describing the destination of their journey, although precise learning objectives are not rigidly specified in advance. Teachers hope to be delighted and amazed by their students' learning.

Grant Wiggins, the former director of research at the CES, described the design features of such 'authentic assessments' as follows:

- They are 'essential'; arbitrary, not unnecessarily intrusive, or designed to produce a mark.
- They are 'facilitative' – constructed to point the learner towards more sophisticated uses of the skills or knowledge.
- They are contextualised, complex intellectual challenges, not 'fragmented' tasks that correspond to isolated 'outcomes'.
- They imply the student's own investigation or use of knowledge, for which the 'content' is a means.
- They assess the habits and repertoires of the student, not mere memorisation or plug-in skills.
- They are representational challenges – designed to emphasise depth rather than breadth.
- They are engaging and instructive.
- They involve somewhat complex tasks or problems.

Given the multidisciplinary nature of the exit exhibition, it is evaluated through a dialogue with the student by a panel of assessors consisting of the learning coach, another expert and a peer (180° feedback). The student is aware of the general criteria by which the presentation/exhibition will be assessed, as these were negotiated at the beginning of the preparation of the task. Approximately 50 minutes are allocated to each exhibition, half of which is spent on the student's presentations and the other half on the discussion with the panel. During the dialogue with the panel, it is expected that probing questions about what has been learned will be discussed, the completed research, reflections on the work covered and its relationship to the wider field, preliminary hypotheses and ideas about further work, and reflections on the learning process itself (meta-learning).

Besides this concrete example, project-based training programmes often show good examples of Assessment-as-Learning in practice. Students often receive continuous feedback on their progress within project work by actively engaging in discussion with their team members and with the client. This works well in authentic 'real-life' projects where there is a customer or an external client. The client's immediate feedback is then an important source of information for defining the next steps within a project. A plan of action and interim reports are perfect input for the evaluation. This answers the following questions: Where are we going, what are the objectives? How far have we got in implementing the project and how are we going to do it exactly? What are the next steps we should take? Final reports and other project results (e.g. a workshop or a final presentation) are the evidence of the learning outcomes of the team. They also provide interesting information that can be used as a basis to reflect and give feedback to each other on what has been learned. This also stimulates future project teamwork and the associated learning process (Dochy et al., 2018).

Within the new concept of 'Assessment-as-Learning', feedback dialogues form the backbone. We conceptualise Assessment-as-Learning as a continuous assessment that is woven into the learning process and consists of 'resource assessment' and 'agency assessment'.

Resource assessment

Resource assessment focuses on evaluating the extent to which and how learners have acquired basic knowledge, skills and competences. Resource assessment encourages the learners to take the next step in deepening and refining the basic knowledge, skills and generic competences step by step. At each step in the learning process, learners use the learning outcomes to demonstrate their developmental progress at an intermediate level of abstraction through the use of rubrics. Portfolio assessment is often used for this purpose and not without reason. Winstone found several studies in which students and instructors indicated that feedback portfolios promote learner independence, encourage reflection and goal setting, facilitate dialogue with coaches and stimulate the search for feedback (Winstone, Nash, Parker, & Rowntree, 2017). In fact, this is pretty much what we want, but variation is very necessary to maintain the impact of learning processes. For this reason, we list 10 more methods that can support resource assessment with multiple assessors:

1. Portfolio assessments (with accountability report and final interview)
2. Two-stage assessments
3. Products as input for assessment
4. Process report as input for assessment
5. 180° feedback
6. 360° feedback

7. Criterion-based interview (determine criteria in interaction with learners)
8. Peer and co-assessment
9. Assessment interviews in team (in which new knowledge is constructed)
10. Assessment interview / final interview individual
11. Exit demonstrations / presentations

Agency assessment

Each assessment method has its advantages and disadvantages and learners often try to anticipate what will be considered in an assessment. Ideally, of course, learners should not think about assessment at all because the integration of learning and assessment is so strong that it feels natural because one is driven to learn. This is a situation we have experienced ourselves and students have been enthusiastic witnesses of this (see also www. highimpactlearningthatlasts.com). However, across cohorts, what assessors look for can also act as signals of 'what is important'. For this reason, James (2012) suggested that 'agency assessment' should also be made explicit. According to James, agency assessment is the assessment of the degree of 'agency' (management) with which one deploys know-how and tools for problem analysis, solution and product-oriented work and one's own evaluation of / reflection on this process. The assurance that is given in the many feedback reports that learners make on the basis of the cyclic feedback dialogues usually provides sufficient information for the learner and assessors to form an accurate picture of this.

For example, in a learning process of a semester, which should encompass about 20 weeks (because no study weeks or test weeks are required), one could have, for example, 20 feedback dialogues, 1 final product and 2 intermediate products, a process report, a 180° feedback, a Criterium-Based Interview (CBI) and 2 peer assessments. That would be 28 data points in a semester that together form the basis for an accurate picture of where the learner stands in his development and what the next steps are.

Feedback as the core of learning   **3**

Central themes

In research on feedback, usually with the implicit or explicit focus on giving feedback, the following three themes are mainly addressed: methods of giving feedback, the quality of the feedback and the response of the feedback recipient. These themes are first addressed in this chapter.

Next, we pay attention to feedback-seeking behaviour, especially in the literature on workplace feedback. Researchers emphasise that a feedback process optimally starts with a feedback request from the learner. Their argument is, in simple terms: unsolicited advice is bad advice.

Finally, we will discuss the different steps in the feedback process.

Methods of giving feedback

Acceptance of feedback is significantly related to the way the feedback is given (Moerkerke, 1996). In their study, Harrison and Rouse (2015) introduced a set of four feedback-giving strategies: (1) personalise, (2) puzzle, (3) measure and (4) prescribe. The first method, personalising, refers to the expression of positive or negative emotional responses (e.g. 'this is wonderful', 'what bothers me most is…') and cognitive responses (e.g. 'this makes me curious'). A second method is puzzling in order to relate back to the receiver what has been observed, often by using an analogy or comparison. Personalisation and puzzling have been conceptualised as informational methods (Harrison & Rouse, 2015; Zhou, 1998). The third method, measurement, is used to express a sense of experience, expertise and authority or to emphasise external or internal norms and expectations. Finally, prescribing is a strategy that provides

DOI: 10.4324/9781003294139-5

direction, explores and encourages change in a specific way. Measuring and prescribing are the two controlling methods where one (manager, teacher) clearly expresses his preference for change (Harrison & Rouse, 2015; Zhou, 1998). Gagné and Deci (2005) argued that individuals are more likely to respond to feedback that is given in a non-controlling way and promotes competence. Steelman and Rutkowski (2004) extended this proposition by recognising that when unfavourable feedback is given in a thoughtful manner, employees are more motivated to improve their performance. Similarly, London (2003) made a distinction between constructive and destructive feedback. He defined constructive feedback as giving concrete information that is useful and is given in a clear and easily understood way. The feedback giver aims to help (i.e. correct, improve or maintain behaviour), and the feedback is interpreted in the same way by the source and the receiver (London, 2003). Destructive feedback, on the other hand, according to London, includes general remarks about performance and attribution of poor performance to internal factors (i.e. the individual himself and not the situational circumstances are the reason for the poor performance). It is given in an inattentive tone and may contain threats (London, 2003). In line with this, Gielen, Dochy and Dierick (2003) state that in feedback the emphasis is on how the learner can proceed and how he can plan his progress.

Finally, and very relevant to practice, already in 1998, Black and William showed that learners take much less account of feedback when it follows a summative assessment with grades. In education, there is a lot of experience with this: students do not show up at a feedback session on a test, they got a six anyway. Learning is no longer important to them; it is only about achieving the minimum score.

The quality of the feedback message

The quality of the feedback message has often been researched and, in addition to the way it is conveyed (see section above), relates to two important characteristics, namely the content (i.e. the type of information, its valence and specificity) and the timing (Kahmann, 2009). The aspect of feedback content concerns the 'what' and provides insight into the type of information, the valence and the specificity of the feedback (Mulder & Ellinger, 2013). Regarding the type of information, feedback should increase knowledge about work- or task-related behaviour (Ilgen, Fisher, & Taylor, 1979; Mulder & Ellinger, 2013). It has been shown that feedback is more effective when it involves information at the task level rather than at the personal level (Hattie & Timperley, 2007; London, 2003). In this regard, Gibbs and Simpson (2004) argue that feedback should focus on the task the learner is performing or the problem, the challenge they are taking up, their learning and the actions over which they are exercising 'agency' and not on the person themselves. They also point out that feedback should be congruent with the goal or end product the learner has in mind (see further: 'feed-up').

With regard to the valence of the feedback sources, Larson (1984) stated that managers have a natural reluctance to give negative feedback, and even experience decision conflicts based on the tension between this reluctance and their role requirements (Larson, Glynn, Fleenor, & Scontrino, 1986). Adams (2005) also suggested that there is a relationship between positive affection and the type of feedback and stated that more valued individuals receive more negative feedback than less valued individuals. Finally, regarding specificity, feedback is more effective when it contains concrete and specific (i.e. detailed) information (Brinko, 1993; Gibbs & Simpson, 2004).

The timing aspect of feedback relates to the 'when' and refers to the time span between the feedback moment and the event or performance to which the feedback relates (Gibbs & Simpson, 2004; Mulder & Ellinger, 2013). Recipients of feedback can use the information when it is given shortly after the discussed event or performance has taken place, because they can connect the feedback to their behaviour. There are findings in research which argue that the effect of the feedback decreases further as more time has passed but also sometimes that the time difference has no significant influence (Mulder & Ellinger, 2013).

The reaction of the feedback recipient

It has been suggested more often that even if the content of the feedback is the same, different individuals may respond in different ways (DeNisi & Sockbeson, 2018). One explanation for the differences in the perception of feedback is that the reaction of the recipient is a function of his motives (does he want to adjust his learning process or does he just want to get good grades?) and of the content of the feedback. This reaction then influences the extent to which and the way in which an individual accepts and further processes the feedback received (Kinicki, Prussia, Wu, & McKee-Ryan, 2004). Three important aspects of the recipient's response are discussed further below: the affective response, the cognitive response and the depth of processing.

The affective response of the recipient

Losada and Heaphy (2004) defined positive feedback as feedback that expresses support, encouragement or appreciation, and negative feedback as feedback that shows disapproval. Belschak and Den Hartog (2009), Ilies, De Pater and Judge (2007) and Wang et al. (2015) found a positive effect of positive feedback on the affective reactions of the feedback recipient. In contrast, negative feedback and criticism often lead to dissatisfaction, defensive reactions, reduced motivation to improve individual performance and less actual improvement in performance (Burke, Weitzel, & Weir, 1978; Jawahar, 2010). Baron (1988) stated that when employees receive destructive criticism, they experience such negative affective reactions (e.g. anger and tension) that they will avoid the feedback source in the future and are highly unlikely to improve their performance. Along the same lines, Jawahar (2010) found that concrete suggestions for improvement as part of the feedback lead to higher satisfaction with the feedback received.

Losada and Heaphy (2004) found that positive and negative feedback also create emotional spaces. Positive feedback creates expansive emotional spaces that open up opportunities for learning. Negative feedback, on the other hand, creates restricted emotional spaces that close off learning. See also similar findings in Voerman et al. (2014). Earlier, Fredrickson (2001) also described similar findings on the constricting influence of negative emotions on a person's momentary thinking and acting repertoire (Losada & Heaphy, 2004).

The cognitive response of the recipient

Ashford (1986) suggested that feedback must first be accepted and internalised before it can be used; that is, cognitive acceptance before the performance can be influenced (Kinicki et al.). Ilgen et al. (1979) defined three main characteristics of the feedback message that lead recipients to perceive the information as accurate and thus accept it: (1) sign, (2) consistency and (3) specificity.

With regard to sign, Ilgen et al. (1979) stated that positive feedback is almost without exception more accepted than negative feedback. According to the findings of Morran, Robison and Stockton (1985), positive feedback is rated higher for content quality and leads to higher feedback acceptance. Individuals perceive positive feedback as more accurate because it better matches what they want to hear and already believe about themselves (Ilgen et al., 1979). Negative feedback, on the other hand, is often perceived as less accurate and therefore less likely to be accepted by the person receiving the feedback (Fedor, Eder, & Buckley, 1989; Steelman & Rutkowski, 2004).

In terms of consistency, Ilgen et al. (1979) argued that feedback that is consistent over time may be more readily accepted.

Finally, regarding specificity, feedback that describes specific incidents and is supported by specific examples is more credible.

In addition to the characteristics of the feedback message, perceived usefulness is also considered crucial for accepting the feedback received. Burke et al. (1978) argued that feedback should be useful and constructive because the recipients would be able to accept and fully use the feedback. Jawahar (2010) also found that suggesting ways to improve performance is positively related to the perceived usefulness of the feedback. Thus, feedback is more likely to be accepted if the feedback is given in a way that promotes the perception of accuracy and usefulness (Kinicki et al., 2004).

Depth of processing

How deeply the feedback information is processed is another relevant response of the feedback receiver. According to Anseel, Lievens and Schollaert (2009), the effectiveness of feedback depends on the depth of processing. Based on the dual-processing models of information processing (Fedor, 1991), one can expect that deeper cognitive processing is related to a better organisation of the feedback information and its integration in long-term memory. This integration in turn makes it easier for feedback recipients to apply the feedback message in subsequent tasks. In contrast, feedback that is inaccurately received or viewed or is only superficially processed has no lasting effects. As a result, the depth of processing could explain why feedback sometimes does not lead to performance improvement (Anseel et al., 2015). In line with these findings, Kluger and DeNisi (1996) proposed in their Feedback Intervention Theory that the effectiveness of feedback depends on the allocation of available cognitive resources and deeper processing of the received information. With regard to the influence of the type of feedback on information processing, a traditional statement in feedback research is that positive feedback is perceived and remembered more accurately than negative feedback (Ilgen, 1971; Ilgen & Hamstra, 1972; Shrauger & Rosenberg, 1970) and one can expect that feedback in dialogue form is much more likely to be processed in depth.

In summary, there are three types of recipient response to the feedback obtained, namely the affective response, the cognitive response and the depth of processing. Regarding the affective reaction, recipients of feedback may experience positive (i.e. satisfaction with the feedback, motivation to improve) or negative (i.e. defensive reaction, negative reaction) emotions to the feedback received. Regarding the cognitive response, an acceptance of the feedback message is more likely if the recipients perceive its accuracy and usefulness as high. Regarding the third type of recipient response, the depth of processing is relevant to the effectiveness of feedback, as processing at a deeper level is associated with better integration and implementation of the received information. These characteristics of the feedback receiver's response are crucial to understand as they can play an important role for the outcomes of feedback exchange and feedback dialogue (e.g. behavioural change, improved performance).

Even though much of this research has been conducted in an outdated context of unidirectional learning processes based on transferring information to a passive listener of learner, we still learned useful things about feedback and the quality of feedback. An overview can be found in Box 3.1.

BOX 3.1

Methods, quality and processing of feedback

Methods of providing feedback

- Feedback at task level is more effective because it increases knowledge of task-related behaviour and reduces uncertainty.
- Feedback is more effective when it contains concrete and specific information. This is referred to as constructive feedback or giving concrete information that is useful and is given in a clear and easily understandable way.
- Learners are more likely to respond to feedback that is given in a non-controlling way and promotes the development of competences.

Quality of the feedback message

- The affective response and emotions of the learner when receiving feedback are determinants of its acceptance and use.
- Positive feedback is linked to positive affective reactions.
- Negative feedback and criticism often lead to dissatisfaction, defensive reactions and less improvement in performance. However, when we give negative feedback in a considerate way, the recipient is more motivated to improve his performance.

(Continued)

- Positive feedback is almost without exception more accepted than negative.
- In terms of timing, receiving feedback shortly after an activity has been performed leads to the recipient of the feedback being more likely to use it than receiving feedback a long time after the activity.
- Concrete suggestions for improvement as part of the feedback lead to higher satisfaction with the feedback received.
- Feedback that is consistent over time is more readily accepted.
- Feedback that describes specific incidents and is supported by specific examples is more credible.
- Feedback that is useful and constructive and is perceived as accurate is better accepted.

Processing of feedback

- Acceptance and internalisation of feedback are necessary before it can lead to adjustment/improvement.
- A favourable interaction between the feedback giver and receiver is important for the response to feedback, acceptance and processing.
- Deeper cognitive processing is important for the use of feedback. A better organisation of the feedback information and its integration in the long-term memory are crucial here. Then, the feedback will also be used in future tasks.
- Feedback in dialogue form has a much greater chance of being processed deeply.

The feedback process

Commonly used terms to describe the feedback process are feed-up, feedback and feedforward (Hattie & Timperley, 2007). They are the three main steps in the feedback process (see Figure 3.1) (to which we will add later on in this book an introductory step called 'connection'; see further).

Feed-up refers to the learner's question with which the feedback process starts: what do I want to achieve? By answering this question, the path the learner wants to take (the learning objectives) becomes transparent, as do the criteria, namely, what quality do I want to achieve and how can you tell if you have delivered quality work. By starting from the learner's question, his/her learning needs, every feedback process is personalised.

Feeding back means that the learner, together with the coach (other people involved in the feedback process), answers the question: how is it going now? Where am I in my process towards the goal I have set? When

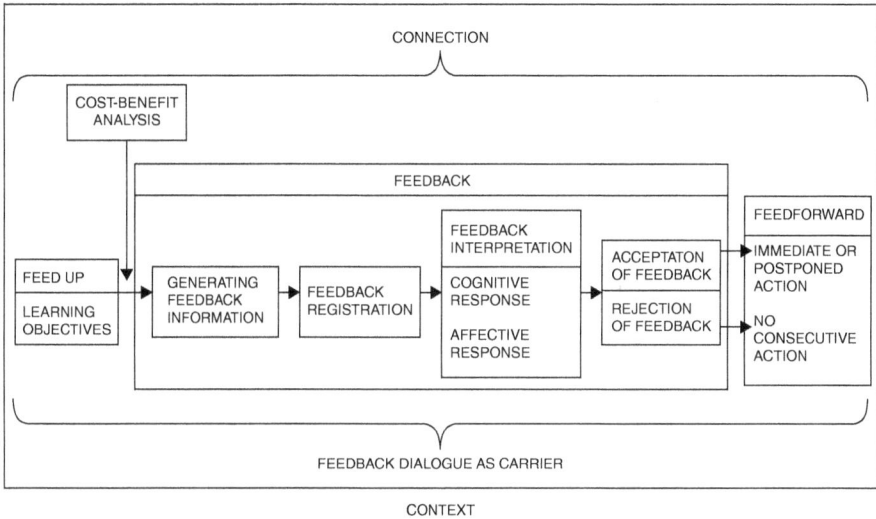

Figure 3.1 Model of the feedback process.

the progress is clear and where one stands now, the question is: What is the next step and how do I take it? This last step can be instigated by the learner or the coach or within their interaction and is called feedforward. By using these questions, you make the learning process clear and transparent. Hattie and Timperley (2007) speak of 'visible learning'. At the same time, these questions are a tool for the learner to steer and regulate the learning process himself; in short, a step towards self-regulation.

Feedback information not only helps the learner to steer the learning process. It is also relevant input for the coach or teacher to check whether the way in which he/she stimulates and facilitates the learner is effective and where adjustments are needed. Because of this use of feedback, namely guiding the learning process and the way in which the coach or teacher stimulates and facilitates, feedback is often associated with the formative function of assessment (Hattie & Timperley, 2007).

In addition to the three steps in the feedback process, Hattie and Timperley (2007) distinguish four feedback levels, or four aspects of the learning process on which feedback can focus: the task, the process, the self-regulation and the level of the self.

- The task level refers to the learning goals that the learner has set.
- Feedback on the process level is about the processes, strategies and thinking paths that the learner needs to achieve his/her goal.

- Feedback on the self-regulating ability of the learner refers to what we previously called 'agency assessment' (see p. 17), namely which (meta) cognitive strategies does the learner use to steer, plan, monitor and evaluate the learning process.
- Feedback at the person-level means giving feedback focused on the person (e.g. 'you're a fast learner', 'you look energetic today', etc.). We have omitted person-level ('self-level') feedback from the Hattie and Timperley model (2007) because we agree with Brooks et al. (2019) that much research has shown that feedback at this level has little to no added value for the learning process.

Other authors such as Price, Handley and Millar (2011); Brooks et al. (2019) and Ashford, Blatt and VandeWalle (2003) outline the feedback process from a different perspective. Price et al. (2011) look at feedback from the question of how to increase student engagement in the learning process through feedback. Brooks et al. start from the Hattie and Timperley (2007) model. Ashford et al. (2003) focus on the search for feedback. We bring these different perspectives together in Figure 3.1.

In summary, we describe the feedback process as follows. The process starts with **feeding up**; that is, the learner sets a goal and wants to achieve something. In order to achieve this goal, he seeks feedback. In this case, we speak of generating feedback in order to better achieve his goal. Whether the learner will actually seek feedback depends on the result of a cost-benefit analysis; that is, is the effort to seek feedback in proportion to the yield I expect from it? If the answer to this question is positive, the learner will seek feedback.

This is where the **feedback** phase starts. The learner will explicitly ask for feedback or retrieve data with a feedback value (e.g. the dashboard in a learning management system that shows the percentage of the learning track that you have completed). He may also seek feedback by observing the reactions of relevant others to his behaviour or performance. This way of seeking feedback often leads to less accurate information because of the room for interpretation.

Next, the learner registers the feedback, records the feedback generated and starts to interpret it. He interprets cognitively, namely what does the feedback mean in terms of achieved goals, the learning process, my self-regulation (see feedback levels of Hattie & Timperley, 2007). He also has an affective reaction to the feedback, namely the feedback is experienced as stimulating or as demotivating. Depending on the interpretation of the feedback, it is accepted, ignored or rejected.

If the feedback is accepted, the learner determines next steps for immediate action or to take action later. This last step is the **feedforward** step.

And from here the feedback process can start again, based on the new goals the learner has set.

The carrier of all the steps in this learning process is dialogue. From setting learning goals to determining next steps, it is through dialogue with relevant others such as the coach or peers, that these steps are more accurate and complete. You will find more information about the feedback dialogue in Part II of this book.

A feedback dialogue is only effective when there is trust between the actors in the dialogue. For this trust to grow, a good connection is needed between the actors. Explicit attention to and work on establishing this connection during all the steps in the feedback dialogue is a condition for the dialogue to be effective.

Finally, the context in which feedback takes place plays a role in increasing involvement. A modular structure, offer of small courses, modules and small units of credits minimise the opportunities and motivation for learners to ask for, give and use feedback. High impact learning programmes work with integrated 'challenges', projects and large units of credits, just to avoid calculating learner behaviour and disinterest in feedback.

The use of rubrics

Rubrics are tools to support assessors in evaluating the quality of the learning process and learning outcomes (Panadero & Jonsson, 2020). A rubric contains criteria, namely which aspects are taken into account in the assessment. In addition, it distinguishes levels of proficiency, describing the learner's behaviour or performance for each criterion and proficiency level. This leads to a two-dimensional matrix with the criteria in the rows, the proficiency levels in the columns and a description of behaviour or performance in the cells. Figure 3.2 shows an example of a rubric that serves as input for the feedback dialogue with the client about the project report (MSc Learning and Development in Organisations, Maastricht University School of Business and Economics).

Since 2007, several review studies have been published on the use of rubrics for formative purposes and their value as input for feedback. The 2013 review by Panadero and Jonsson shows that there is considerable evidence on the value of using rubrics for transparency in formative assessment of students, reducing student anxiety about the assessment process, making the feedback process more effective, supporting student self-regulation and indirectly improving learning outcomes through this route. These findings were confirmed in the review study by Brookhart and Chen (2015).

Performance criteria	Novice	Developing	Experienced	Professional
1. Accessibility of the report and, if relevant, other deliverables	Too poor to be communicated in the organization. Writing style makes the report inaccessible for the reader: ideas and paragraphs are disjointed and do not flow smoothly; very frequent and major referencing, grammatical and spelling errors; presence of colloquialisms and logical sequence errors.	Ready for communication in the organization, however after major revisions. Parts of the report flow smoothly, others are disjointed; parts of the report show major grammatical, spelling, referencing, logical sequence errors and/or colloquialisms. In sum: major revisions needed.	Ready for communication in the organization, however after minor revisions. Report generally flows smoothly but is a bit brief (or 'wordy') in places; generally the report has some minor referencing, spelling, grammatical, logical sequence errors and/or colloquialisms. In sum: minor revisions needed.	Ready for communication in the organization. Report is easy to read, logical and flows smoothly from issues to conclusions. The presentation is competent without referencing, spelling, logical sequence, grammatical errors and/or colloquialisms. In sum: no revisions needed.
	☐	☐	☐	☐

Main strong points:

Main suggestions for improvement:

Performance criteria	Novice	Developing	Experienced	Professional
2. Insights and recommendations offered in the report and, if relevant, in other deliverables	No value to the organization. The description and analysis of the main project questions as well as the recommendations offered miss a clear and accurate argumentation and do not fit the specific context of the organization. It is not clear if choices between alternatives are made and why.	Value to the organization, however some major revisions are needed in terms of elaboration and argumentation of formulation of project questions, analysis and recommendations. It is not yet fully clear why choices are made (or not made) and there is still major work to do to make insights and recommendations applicable to the organization. In sum: major revisions needed.	Value to the organization, however some minor revisions are needed in terms of elaboration and argumentation of description of project questions, analysis and recommendations. There is minor work to do to make clear why choices are made (or not made) and to make insights and recommendations applicable to the organization. In sum: minor revisions needed.	Excellent value to the organization. Excellent elaboration and argumentation of project questions, their analysis and the recommendations formulated. Accurate and clear argumentation of choices made (or not made); analysis as well as recommendations are applicable to the organization. In sum: no revisions needed.
	☐	☐	☐	☐

Main strong points:

Main suggestions for improvement:

Performance criteria	Novice	Developing	Experienced	Professional
3. Project management	Rarely or never used time wisely to complete project tasks/activities. Turned in no draft and final project deliverables on or before the due date.	Occasionally used time wisely but usually procrastinated in completing. Turned in most draft and final project deliverables on or before the due date.	Usually used time wisely to complete project tasks/ activities but may have procrastinated occasionally. Turned in most draft and final project deliverables on time.	Consistently used time wisely to complete project tasks/activities. Turned in all draft and final project deliverables on time.
	☐	☐	☐	☐

Main strong points:

Main suggestions for improvement:

Figure 3.2 Rubrics. *(Continued)*

Performance criteria	Novice	Developing	Experienced	Professional
4. Client interaction	A clear lack of accurate and on-time planning of meetings; no preparation of the meetings; a lack of accurate follow up of action points decided upon during meetings; no use of resources (data, information, facilities, people etc) made available to the team; no transparent and respectful communication about the project progress and about issues that cropped up during the execution of the project.	Occasionally accurate and on-time planning of meetings; occasionally well prepared for the meetings; occasionally accurate follow up of action points decided upon during meetings; use of resources (data, information, facilities, people etc) made available by the client can be significantly improved; occasionally transparent and respectful communication about the project progress and about issues that cropped up during the execution of the project.	Usually accurate and on-time planning of meetings; usually well prepared for the meetings; usually transparent and respectful communication; usually accurate follow up of action points decided upon during meetings; appropriate use of resources (data, information, facilities, people etc) made available by client; regular transparent and respectful communication about the project progress and about issues that cropped up during the execution of the project.	Consistently accurate and on-time planning of meetings; well prepared for the meetings; consistently transparent and respectful communication; consistently accurate follow up of action points decided upon during meetings; excellent use of resources (data, information, facilities, people etc) made available by client; consistently transparent and respectful communication about the project progress and about issues that cropped up during the execution of the project.
	☐	☐	☐	☐
Main strong points:				
Main suggestions for improvement:				

Rationale for final grade:	
<5.5	quality indicators mainly scored on lowest level (novice)
>=5.5, <7	quality indicators mainly scored on second level (developing)
>7.0, <=8.5	quality indicators mainly scored on third level (experienced)
> 8.5	quality indicators mainly scored on fourth level (professional)

Figure 3.2 (Continued)

In addition to positive effects, many studies also point to negative consequences of using rubrics. Panadero and Jonsson (2020) brought these studies together and analysed the quality of the reported evidence. This analysis leads to the following findings. A first criticism of the use of rubrics is that they sometimes capture complex behaviour or complex competences in oversimplified criteria or inadequate criteria (i.e. not a sufficient representation of the assessed competence). In short, the competence that is the subject of the feedback is too complex to be captured in a limited number of or simply formulated criteria. Panadero and Jonsson (2020) rightly point out that the rubric is only a tool that provides input to the feedback dialogue and in particular the conversation is necessary for nuances, floors, and broadenings of the assessment. A second criticism is that the use leads to instrumental learning or 'criteria compliance' and thus encourages students to 'take the path of least resistance' or 'score quickly'. Panadero and Jonsson (2020) argue that the way the rubric is used in the feedback dialogue plays a positive role in how students interact with rubrics. The third critique aligns with Panadero and Jonsson's (2020) counter-arguments, namely, simple implementation of rubrics does not work.

Feedback literacy

Interaction and dynamic feedback from experts is necessary to enable learners to improve their work by interacting in order to come to a plan of action based on the feedforward. Such expert help should certainly not revert to the transmission model by lecturing and training learners in feedback literacy. Rather, it is crucial that learners experience continuous feedback dialogue in practice.

Based on Evans (2013), we formulate the following conditions that are necessary for seeking feedback to actually lead to learning gains:

a. the focus of the learner is on learning, development and giving meaning;
b. the learner has the skills to take control of his own learning process;
c. the learner is able to interpret feedback;
d. the learner can recognise opportunities and make the most of them;
e. the learner has resilience (self-awareness and self-monitoring);
f. the learner has the ability to manage their own personal response to feedback;
g. the learner can take responsibility in the feedback and feed-forward process;
h. the learner has the skills to transfer and adapt the feedback generated to different contexts.

Does this mean that feedback seeking is only for the 'happy few'? No. Practice makes perfect. Frequent feedback dialogues as part of the daily learning process help the learner to become feedback literate, as Carless and Boud (2018) call it.

Interaction and dynamic feedback from others, such as a coach and peers, helps learners develop the skills Evans (2013) identifies as a prerequisite for effective feedback-seeking behaviour.

Sustainable feedback

According to Carless and colleagues, sustainable feedback includes the following four characteristics (Carless, Salter, Yang, & Lam, 2011):

- engaging learners in dialogues about learning that make them aware of what constitutes quality processes and performance,
- develop learners in monitoring their own learning,
- develop learners' capacities for lifelong learning by supporting them in developing skills such as goal-setting and planning and

- stimulate learners' engagement over time, generating, processing and using feedback from different sources to improve processes and performance step by step during the challenges they are working on.

What Carless and colleagues (2011) see clearly is that much more needs to be done in terms of communication (e.g. about the purpose of feedback and its central role in the process). Even though they place a clear focus on the role of self-regulation as a prerequisite for sustainable feedback, what they overlook is that strong self-regulation of one's own learning is not possible in a situation where a teacher does not coach, but rather directs, tests and monitors, and thus does not maximise learner agency. Dialogic interaction, peer feedback and self-evaluation are what learners should do and learn from the progression. Sustainable feedback focuses to an important extent on learner agency and specifically on the extent to which the learner regulates his learning process (see also Leaner Agency, Chapter 8). We do agree with David Carless that improved self-regulating capacities as a result of sustainable feedback will lead to better quality of learning and performance (Carless et al., 2011).

Feedback-seeking behaviour   **4**

What is feedback-seeking behaviour?

The feedback dialogue begins with an individual proactively seeking to obtain feedback information (Butler & Winne, 1995; Nakai & O'Malley, 2015). In the feedback literature, this is called 'feedback seeking' and it was first articulated by Ashford and Cummings (1983), who challenged the traditional view of the feedback seeker as passively waiting for feedback (Ilgen, Fischer, & Taylor, 1979). They introduced the proactive notion of feedback seeking and defined it as 'the conscious commitment of effort to determine the appropriateness and adequacy of behaviour for the achievement of valued end states and goals' (Ashford, 1986, p. 466). Since then, the concept of feedback seeking has been further developed in the literature, however mainly from an individual, one-sided perspective. In their literature review, Ashford, Blatt and VandeWalle (2003) identified five main patterns of feedback seeking: method, frequency, timing, source characteristics and topic.

Methods of generating feedback

Ashford and Cummings identified two main feedback-seeking strategies, inquiry and monitoring (1983). Inquiry refers to the explicit verbal request for information, while monitoring is an indirect method in which the source and the environment are observed for clues about how one is doing (Ashford et al., 2003). Ashford and Cummings (1983) argued that the decision on which search strategy to use depends on different motives and situations.

DOI: 10.4324/9781003294139-6

For example, if professionals are driven by an instrumental motive (e.g. the motive to achieve s certain goal), they would seek feedback through a direct enquiry guided by the high diagnostic value of the feedback (Tuckey, Brewer, & Williamson, 2002). On the contrary, individuals driven by the image motive (e.g. the motive to enhance or protect one's image in an organisation) would likely use indirect search strategies (i.e. monitoring) to avoid loss of face and a bad impression (Anseel, Lievens, & Levy, 2007).

Frequency and timing

Other aspects of seeking feedback that research has focused on are the frequency and timing of the search attempt. Frequency refers to how often individuals seek feedback (Ashford et al., 2003). According to Ashford and Northcraft (1992), individuals use norms about typical feedback-seeking behaviour as cues to decide how often they seek feedback. Norms suggesting that feedback seeking is frequent promote more frequent feedback seeking and vice versa (Ashford & Northcraft, 1992). Furthermore, the motives for seeking feedback are an essential determinant of how often to seek feedback. According to Ashford et al. (2003), the instrumental motive increases the frequency of seeking feedback because of the high diagnostic value of the information received. On the contrary, Ashford and Northcraft (1992) suggested that professionals guided by the image motive who consider using impression management strategies would seek feedback less frequently when seeking is public than when it is private. In addition to these factors, Ashford (1986) suggested that organisational tenure is negatively related to the frequency with which employees seek feedback. Thus, professionals who have been in office longer tend to seek feedback less frequently. Also, individuals who value feedback about their performance were found to request it more often (Ashford, 1986).

Timing of feedback-seeking behaviour refers to the length of time between an event (e.g. task performance, behaviour) and the attempt to obtain event-specific feedback (VandeWalle, 2003). In other words, it indicates whether an individual sought feedback immediately after a performance-related event or with a delay. Professionals strategically determine when they seek feedback and the literature distinguishes between immediate and delayed feedback (e.g. Hattie & Timperley, 2007). Reid and Parsons (1996) found that all professionals who participated in staff training preferred immediate over delayed feedback. Morrison and Bies (1991) found that employees who are guided by impression management (i.e. an image-based motive) were more likely to seek feedback after positive than after negative events.

Individuals who are guided by the instrumental motive are more likely to seek feedback soon after a relevant event because immediate feedback rather than delayed feedback is related to higher performance (Mulder & Ellinger, 2013).

What influences the feedback giver?

Several studies have focused on examining the attributions that managers make when they are asked for feedback. Lam, Huang and Snape (2007) provided an important insight by showing that source ratings are influenced by two of the motives underlying feedback-seeking behaviour, namely the instrumental and the image-based motive. By examining 499 manager-subordinate dyads engaged in a feedback exchange, Lam et al. (2007) found that when managers attribute employee feedback seeking to the instrumental motive, they also tend to evaluate their work performance more positively. This more positive evaluation also applies to the quality of the relationship between the feedback giver and the feedback seeker. The impression-management attributions of supervisors are negatively related to the perceived quality of the relationship between supervisor-subordinate and the job performance of the seeker (Lam et al., 2007). Interestingly, the authors also argued that it is not the real motives of the seeker that are relevant, but the attributions of the giver. For example, if a supervisor attributes search behaviour to impression management, the type of feedback given will reflect this interpretation, even if the employee seeks feedback based on the instrumental motive.

Moreover, Ashford and Northcraft (1992) emphasised that feedback seekers with a history of average performance are evaluated less favourably than feedback seekers with a history of superior performance. An explanation for this difference in evaluation is given by DeNisi, Cafferty and Meglino (1984), who suggested that feedback seekers pay attention to salient information when they evaluate the behaviour of professionals. In his 1920 research, Thorndike suggested that a salient cue (i.e. the performance history of the feedback seeker) could serve as a halo effect. Thus, the salient cue influences the source interpretation of the specific search behaviour in a way that is consistent with it (De Stobbeleir, Ashford, & de Luque, 2010). As a result, managers are likely to interpret the feedback search attempt of superior performers as a sign of their striving for improvement and thus gain a more favourable view of their potential and individual characteristics (Ashford & Northcraft, 1992). However, managers are less likely to make the same attribution for employees with a history of average performance (De Stobbeleir et al., 2010).

DeNisi and Sockbeson (2018) introduced another concept that determines feedback-giving behaviour, namely the giver's anticipation of being asked for feedback at the time of the questioning. The authors argue that when sources expect to be asked for feedback, they are more likely to process the feedback information through online processing. Online processing implies that feedback providers form judgements based on the recipient's performance-related events and update them in the process (DeNisi & Sockbeson, 2018). According to the authors, this approach results in better recall of specific performance information, making it more valuable and useful because it guides certain behaviour. In contrast, when feedback providers do not expect to be asked for feedback, they rely more on memory-based processing, resulting in better recall of the employee's overall performance (DeNisi & Sockbeson, 2018). The authors argue that memory-based processing generates less useful feedback than online processing because the attitudes formed are weaker and the certainty is lower.

Characteristics of the source (or feedback giver)

The characteristics of the feedback source (i.e. the feedback giver) have also been found to influence the seeking of feedback and the acceptance of the feedback received (Ilgen et al., 1979; Tuckey, Brewer, & Barnes, 2006). This implies the importance of source characteristics for feedback dialogue. According to Vancouver and Morrison (1995), there are four central source characteristics (i.e. attributes), namely (1) expertise, (2) accessibility, (3) reward power and (4) relationship quality.

Source expertise refers to the level of technical knowledge and skills of the source, which is relevant to the searcher's performance (Ilgen et al., 1979; Klich & Feldman, 1992). Expertise has been shown to be positively related to feedback-seeking behaviour, not only when it is defined solely in terms of skills and knowledge, but also when it includes expertise in being good at giving positive and negative feedback (Amah, 2008). More so, the motives for seeking feedback influence the decision of whom to seek feedback from in the sense that individuals guided by the instrumental motive will choose more experienced sources. More specifically, the more expertise a source has, the higher the instrumental value of its feedback, and thus the more likely individuals are to seek feedback from this person (Vancouver & Morrison, 1995).

Accessibility is defined as the expected ease with which the feedback seeker can access and use a particular source (Morrison & Vancouver, 2000). The authors argue that the more accessible the source, the more people will be inclined to seek feedback from it. Borgatti and Cross (2003) emphasised that the expertise of a source is not enough and that the accessibility of the source is an essential condition to truly benefit from the situation in which feedback is sought.

The third source characteristic, having the power to give rewards (rewarding power), is high when the feedback source is perceived to have control over desired positive outcomes (Amah, 2008). Furthermore, Amah (2008) showed that high reward power is positively related to feedback-seeking behaviour. This indicates that in a High Impact Learning that Lasts (HILL) context, it is important that assessors of outcomes, processes and products are diverse: peers, coach, external client and so on. In this way, they all meet the requirements of the HILL. In this way, they all fulfil the criterion of rewarding power, because even if we no longer work with scores, a learner will seek reward, recognition and so on in a different way.

Finally, the fourth source characteristic lies in the quality of the relationship between the feedback seeker and the feedback giver. Given its importance for the feedback dialogue, it is conceptualised as another feedback dialogue characteristic (relational dependence).

Motives for seeking feedback

Traditionally, three main motives for seeking feedback are distinguished in the literature: (1) instrumental motive, (2) ego-based motive and (3) image-based motive (Ashford & Cummings, 1983). The instrumental motive is used by individuals because of its informational value, which helps them to achieve their goals and regulate their behaviour (Ashford, 1986; Ashford & Tsui, 1991). Previous studies indicate that feedback has a particularly high instrumental value in uncertain situations; it is therefore expected that individuals will request feedback more frequently under these circumstances (Ashford et al., 2003).

The second motive underlying feedback-seeking behaviour, the ego-based motive, relates to the individual's self-image (Northcraft & Ashford, 1990). Feedback seekers who are driven by this motive do not interpret the information received in a neutral way, because information about the self is emotionally charged (Ashford et al., 2003). As a result, their feelings of self-worth, self-esteem and self-confidence are threatened (Anseel et al., 2007). Therefore, an important hypothesis in the literature on feedback seeking is that individuals will avoid seeking feedback when it may threaten their ego (Anseel et al., 2007). For example, Northcraft and Ashford (1990) argued that professionals with low performance expectations seek less feedback than those with high expectations. Moreover, Ashford and Cummings (1983) argued that the ego-based motive may encourage feedback seeking to reinforce a positive self-image (ego-enhancement motive) or discourage it to avoid ego threats (ego-defence motive).

Finally, the image motive is used to enhance and protect the image of individuals in the organisation or group (Anseel et al., 2007). The authors argue that individuals are sensitive to the opinions of others and want to maintain a positive image in public. Similar to the ego-based motive, Morrison and Bies (1991) indicate that the image-based motive can help individuals to improve their public image (i.e. enhancement motive) or to protect it (i.e. defence motive). The difference between ego and image motives is that the ego-based motive is rather inward looking, whereas the image-based motive is more outward looking (Hays & Williams, 2011). Although this motive can also contribute to image enhancement, in feedback-seeking research it has been mainly recognised as a motive to avoid feedback, as individuals are more likely to not seek feedback in order to avoid loss of face (Anseel et al., 2007).

Subject of the feedback looked for

Depending on the context, feedback seekers can decide for themselves the subject of the feedback they seek. This is particularly true in learning environments where learner agency is central. When learner agency is more of a dead letter and the culture in the programme is controlling and one-sidedly performance-oriented (i.e. with little or no learning orientation), we often see undesirable effects of letting the learner determine the feedback request himself. Several researchers have pointed out, for example, that individuals act strategically when they seek feedback (Ashford & Tsui, 1991) and tactically decide on what topic to seek information (e.g. Ashford et al., 2003). As Ashford and Tsui (1991) argue, professionals may strategically focus on one topic over another to gather more positive or negative feedback. They selectively seek feedback that improves their social image, for example by seeking only positive feedback on their performance and avoiding negative feedback on poor performance (Morrison & Bies, 1991). These findings suggest that the subject of the feedback sought depends strongly on the motive underlying the desire for feedback. Although it is certainly good for learner agency that learners themselves determine the topics they want to talk about in the feedback dialogue, it is also natural in such a dialogue for the other parties to propose topics that can lead to deeper learning.

An overview can be found in Box 4.1.

BOX 4.1
_____

Summary of seeking feedback

- Visible norms in the organisation suggesting that seeking feedback is frequent promote more frequent seeking of feedback.
- Instrumentality/utility increases the frequency of asking for feedback.
- Learners who value feedback ask for it more often.
- Professionals are more likely to ask for feedback immediately (because they value it).
- Seeking behaviour is influenced by (1) expertise (we are more likely to seek out an expert), (2) accessibility (especially accessible individuals are more likely to be queried), (3) rewarding ability (those with rewarding ability are more likely to be queried) and (4) relationship quality (a good relationship stimulates the frequency of querying).
- An instrumental motive (information value) stimulates feedback-seeking behaviour.
- If learners themselves determine the subject(s) of feedback, this stimulates their 'learner agency'.

Types of feedback   **5**

In the literature, experts describe not only generic characteristics of feedback but also different types of feedback. There are many types of feedback and they are too many to be able to use them clearly in practice. We will only discuss the most relevant types for us here.

First of all, the vision that one has of feedback is related to the vision of learning and this influences the type of feedback. We then compare feedback from a cognitivist, socio-constructivist, connectivist perspective and from the perspective of hybrid expansionism. Next, we distinguish different types of feedback based on the sources of feedback and, finally, briefly discuss E-feedback.

Types of feedback based on the view of learning and feedback

According to Evans (2013), a distinction is often made between a cognitivist and a socio-constructivist view of feedback, but of course there is also a more recent connectivist view and the now very current hybrid expansivist view of feedback.

The cognitivist perspective is closely linked to a directive approach in which feedback is seen as corrective, in which an expert gives the correct information to the passive recipient.

From the socio-constructivist paradigm, feedback is rather seen as a facilitative approach, where comments and suggestions are given to allow students to make their own revisions and where students are helped to gain new insights without dictating what those insights will be.

DOI: 10.4324/9781003294139-7

However, constructivism also emerged half a century ago, at a time when there was no such thing as information density, information speed, networks and so on. Not only has the whole of society changed dramatically since then, but young people and learners in general have different views and habits.

More recently, the connectivist view of learning and feedback has emerged, which reflects the dynamic nature of learning, where the coach also learns from the student through dialogue and participation in shared experiences (Carless, Salter, Yang, & Lam, 2011). In such situations, connections between participants in learning communities lead to shared understandings as part of the development of communities of practice (Wenger, McDermott, & Synder, 2002). The complexity of networks is then a challenge in giving, taking and adapting feedback. Connectivism indicates that learning is a process of connecting sources and networks in which the capacity to acquire knowledge is more important than what someone can reproduce at a given time (Dochy, Gijbels, Segers, & Van den Bossche, 2022).

Currently, **hybrid expansivism** (Dochy et al., 2022) is taken as the starting point, in which expansive learning (creating new knowledge), hybrid learning and 'learner agency' are central and where learning is based on continuous feedback or Assessment-as-Learning as an extension of connectivism. Here, the learner takes greater responsibility for seeking and acting on feedback, which is always generated in dialogue with the coach (and peers) and is cyclical in nature.

In the literature, the emphasis for years was on feedback as a corrective instrument, whereas it should now be seen primarily as a means of creating challenges and offering self-confidence. This also leads to impact.

Types of feedback based on the feedback sources

We distinguish between 90°, 180° or 360° feedback, self-feedback and peer feedback.

90°, 180° or 360° feedback

Feedback by a certain number of 'degrees' refers to the number of different 'persons' involved in the feedback process. The number of persons participating in the feedback dialogue increases with the number of degrees. In a 90° feedback, the learner is scanned for the mastery of competences by himself and the coach. The difference with a traditional assessment interview is that space is given to the learner to reflect on his own result and the route to it and to give feedback on the coach's way of coaching. It is therefore a reciprocal process. The coach and learner know where they stand, what they think about each other's performance and whether they understand each other's feedback. These are essential conditions for bringing implicit emotions or thoughts to the surface and preventing (sometimes lingering) conflicts (Dochy & Nickmans, 2005).

In 180° feedback, a competence scan is carried out by the learner, a 'peer' (fellow student, colleague) and the coach or alternatively the learner, the coach and an external party (e.g. the problem owner, customer or client). In a 360° feedback, four parties are involved; learner, coach, peer and external. There is then a discussion of the process and the product or performance from four different perspectives. Especially in the business world, the latter method is often used to evaluate the professional performance of staff members. The term 360° feedback was launched in 1973 by the consulting group 'Teams Inc.' in Miami. As the term 360° feedback already indicates, feedback is the active ingredient of this method: there is feedback in dialogue from different perspectives on the development of competence (Dochy & Nickmans, 2005). It is basically a combination of self-, peer- and co-assessment, an evaluation from multiple sources. In a 360° feedback, each assessor uses certain quality criteria that he/she believes are relevant. The basic idea of this method is that no absolute agreement is required between assessors. Involving different perspectives, values and quality criteria in the assessment process provides a more accurate picture of the learner's competences (Dochy & Nickmans, 2005). The learner gains insight into how effectiveness and quality are perceived by other relevant parties. He is confronted with a possible discrepancy between the way he sees himself and the way others see him. This approach ensures that the assessment is more in-depth and often more nuanced, therefore more likely to be accepted, and provides stronger motivation to continue working on competence development.

Self-feedback

Self-feedback can be seen as the most formative use of self-assessment, in which learners create their own feedback, focused as much as possible on content accuracy and on development of expertise. Self-feedback is often used as a synonym for reflection. It is an important part of a feedback dialogue. Usually such a dialogue starts with a question like 'How did it go?' or 'What did you think of it?' and 'Where did it go well and where not?'.

This self-generated feedback can lead to a reinterpretation of the task or assignment being worked on, the predetermined learning objectives and/or the method of approach. Self-feedback is therefore an important element of self-regulated learning, the constructive process by which a learner sets goals, charts a path to achieve them and monitors this path and the cognitions, emotions and behaviours involved (Panadero, Lipnevich, & Broadbent, 2019; Pintrich & Zusho, 2002).

Just as self-regulated learning is a developmental process, the ability to question and give feedback is something we develop (Parker & Baughan, 2011). Research has consistently shown that interventions aimed at developing self-feedback have a positive effect on learners' self-regulation and self-efficacy (Andrade, 2019). Recent literature has described and compared a variety of tools to support self-feedback. Kori, Pedaste, Leijen and Mäeots (2014), for example, analysed technical tools for self-feedback in technology-enhanced learning environments. An important conclusion is that even though tools such as videos, blogs or portfolios play a relevant role in the development of self-feedback, human interaction (e.g. with a coach) is crucial. It also appears that some people need more support than others (Alkaher & Dolan, 2011).

An important starting point is an explicit positive perception by learners of the value of self-feedback and their previous positive experiences (Boud & Falchikov, 2007). Furthermore, a collaborative learning environment obviously supports the stimulation of self-regulation and self-feedback, that is a HILL environment with a lot of interaction based on a positive mindset and a positive learning climate. After all, learning is highly contagious.

Evans (2013) mentions some successful approaches to promote self-regulation and facilitate self-feedback, for example:

- students assigning their own grade based on feedback from instructors (and peers) and justifying it in 100 words (Sendzuik, 2010);
- assessments where students assess their own competence, then perform specific tasks, get an expert's view on them and then prepare their own comparative paper (Jonsson, Mattheos, Svingby, & Attstrom, 2007); and
- self-revised essays where students develop their work based on all sources of feedback obtained both formally and informally (Graziano-King, 2007).

These approaches demonstrate the central role of the learner in authentic situations where he/she demonstrates the ability to apply acquired competence to solve real-life problems.

Peer feedback

We have previously defined peer feedback as 'an arrangement whereby individuals consider the quantity, level, value, quality or success of the products or learning outcomes of peers of comparable status' (Gielen, Dochy, et al., 2011 p. 137). It is therefore information given to the learners that is intended to change their thinking or behaviour in order to improve their learning (Shute, 2008).

Peer feedback has also been extensively researched in previous scientific research (Dochy, Segers, & Sluijsmans, 1999; Falchikov & Goldfinch, 2000; Gielen, Dochy, & Onghena, 2011; Gielen et al., 2010; Panadero, 2016; Panadero, Jonsson, & Botella, 2017; Topping, 1998; Van Gennip, Segers, & Tillema, 2009; Wiliam, 2011).

In our 2011 publication, we showed that peer feedback can serve five purposes: social control tool, assessment tool, learning tool, tool for learning how to assess and tool for active participation (Gielen, Dochy, et al., 2011). In a high-impact learning context, peer feedback will primarily fulfil a function as a tool for active participation in the learning process, an opportunity to understand the feedback process and become proficient at it, and above all as a learning instrument or to expand and deepen knowledge, skills and competencies. Van Gennip, Segers and Tillema (2010) therefore describe peer feedback as a form of collaborative learning. In a learning environment where collaborative learning is central, peer feedback is inherent to the learning process. The roles of seeking and giving feedback and the entire feedback process are a 'natural' part of the interaction between learners. When interaction in peer feedback is central and peer feedback is thus dialogical, both the giver and the receiver in the peer feedback process achieve learning gains. Liu and Carless (2006, p. 281) describe the learning gain for the feedback giver as follows: 'students develop objectivity in relation to standards which can then be transferred to their own work'. This is confirmed by Evans (2013) who concludes on the basis of a literature review that receiving feedback has less effect on future performance than giving feedback.

What are the effects of peer feedback?

Overall, the results of the Wisniewski, Zierer and Hattie (2020) meta-analysis into the effects of feedback on student learning indicate that, in terms of the direction of feedback between parties, student-student feedback is the most effective form (Wisniewski et al., 2020). Double, McGrane and Hopfenbeck (2020) also concluded from their quantitative review that:

'The results suggest that peer assessment improves academic performance compared with no assessment (g = 0.31, p = .004) and teacher assessment (g = 0.28, p = .007)'. Of course, they find differences depending on whether the peer feedback is online or offline, depending on frequency or educational level. They conclude that the effectiveness of peer feedback is remarkably robust across a wide range of contexts. In contrast to these studies, Gielen, Tops, et al. (2010) showed that there were no significant differences between teacher feedback and peer feedback in terms of student progress. Huisman, Saab, van den Broek and van Driel (2019) confirmed this finding in their meta-analysis on effects of teacher feedback and peer feedback in writing instruction. At the same time, Wu and Schunn (2020) indicate that peer feedback has a number of advantages over teacher feedback, namely that it is faster, more detailed and easier to understand.

Liu and Carless (2006) compare peer assessment, which they describe as peers giving grades for summative purposes, and peer feedback (formative purposes) and conclude that peer feedback has a more substantial effect on learning than peer assessment.

More specifically, researchers indicate that peer feedback is motivating; it helps the development of metacognition; it teaches learners to monitor their own progress and that of others, to adapt strategies, to improve communication and interpersonal skills and to develop a sense of self-control (Ballantyne, Hughes, & Mylonas, 2002). Moreover, it is an important stimulus for the development of lifelong learning competence and self-assessment skills (Topping, 2010; Xiao & Lucking, 2008). In addition, studies show that peer feedback leads to greater learner agency (Yang, Badger, & Yu, 2006) and that teacher feedback results in more learner passivity and dependence (Lee, 2008).

Some authors (e.g. Vedder, 1985) explain the positive effects of peer feedback as follows. Peers use a common language, experience similar problems and share an identical living environment. Peers experience and observe problems, ambiguities and misconceptions personally, while experts are much further removed from them.

Next to the positive effects of using feedback, some researchers also point to a negative effect such as discomfort among learners that can appear in some cases (Papinczak, Young, & Groves, 2007).

When is peer feedback effective?

Panadero, Jonsson and Alqassab (2018) showed research findings demonstrating that practice and previous experience is a crucial factor in increasing the quality of feedback that students provide to each other.

Gielen, Tops, et al. (2010) also showed that an extended peer feedback system (i.e. where students were encouraged to respond to the feedback they had received) was superior to both the 'simple' peer feedback condition (i.e. without encouragement to react to their feedback) and the teacher feedback condition, in terms of student progress.

In order to come to effective feedback, Van Gennip et al. (2010) demonstrated the importance of an atmosphere of trust and psychological safety rather than competition for grades.

Based on a review of the literature, Evans (2013) lists the following conditions for effective feedback:

- Peer feedback from multiple peers is preferred because multiple observations make the picture more complete. Therefore, peer feedback from multiple peers is more accurate.
- Peer feedback is most effective when included as an element within a holistic assessment.
- How peer feedback is implemented and what the exact role of the assessor and the person being assessed is influence the effects of peer feedback.
- The academic ability of the feedback giver and receiver has an influence.
- Not all learners are positive about peer feedback. The learner's choice of peer feedback is important.
- Peer feedback has more value when it is used for formative rather than summative purposes.
- The nature and type of feedback given by peers affects its impact.
- Peer feedback requires skills that can be developed through practice.

Finally, we would like to emphasise that peer feedback, like feedback in general, is a process, whereby feedback is generated, given, processed and used. Bangert-Drowns, Kulik, Kulik and Morgan (1991) and Bolzer, Strijbos and Fischer (2015) emphasise the importance of 'mindful reception' and 'mindful processing'. By this, they refer to how deeply peer feedback is cognitively understood and processed. Mindful processing is in line with previous studies by Kluger and DeNisi (1996) and Anseel et al. (2015) who indicate that in addition to the cognitive and affective response to the generated feedback, the depth of the response influences the effectiveness of peer feedback.

E-feedback

Evans (2013, p. 85) defines e-feedback as follows: 'E-assessment feedback (EAF) includes formative and summative feedback delivered or conducted through information communication technology of any kind, encompassing various digital technologies including CD-ROM, television, interactive multimedia, mobile phones, and the Internet'. E-feedback can be asynchronous or synchronous, face to face or remote, include automated or personalised feedback and can be directed to the individual or a group/team.

In Evans' (2013) review, over 100 articles focused on E-feedback showed that the effect of E-feedback interventions varied widely. However, this was also true for traditional one-way feedback. According to Gilbert, Whitelock and Gale (2011), this is not due to the e-feedback interventions themselves but the crucial aspect is whether an improved learning approach has been introduced. A key factor in the effectiveness of e-feedback technologies is the nature of the interaction between the learner and coach. Also wasn't it the same for ordinary feedback? Here again, the star aspect of dialogue is the crucial factor that determines whether learners understand the feedback, develop an action plan based on the feedback and so on. The use of e-feedback does not automatically imply a change in the roles, autonomy and power relationship between learner and coach. Therefore, it will not automatically lead to effect either.

E-feedback runs the risk of quickly becoming similar to traditional written feedback (but on an electronic medium) where we know the effects are minimal or non-existent. E-feedback is therefore a good alternative if it meets all the conditions of our model for dialogic feedback.

In practice, this will lead to a fine variety of work for the various parties involved by conducting a dialogue via audio or video chat. Making a recording can then support the learner in summarising the feedback and making a step-by-step plan.

Technological tools to stimulate and facilitate feedback and so on are being used more and more. For example, students value personalised audio feedback (Parkes & Fletcher, 2017). Both increased engagement and increased number of times viewing or listening to audio or video feedback are observed (Brearley & Cullen, 2012). Learning analytics also enable information from portfolios and digital traces to provide timely, personalised feedback. This also increases learners' satisfaction with feedback processes (Pardo et al., 2017).

According to Carless and Boud (2018), risks from the technology are certainly the continued provision of feedback as corrective (resulting in little or no effect), and the lack of agency from learners and the lack of productive action.

An overview of commonly used online feedback tools can be found in Part IV of this book.

The impact of feedback   **6**

From the 1990s onwards, we regularly attended the 'World Assessment for Learning' Meeting, an initiative of Rick Stiggins from ETS to which he invited five experts from each continent. We represented the assessment experts of Europe, together with Linda Allal, Kari Smith and Menucha Birenbaum. Besides European experts, British ('experts from non-continental Europe' they were called) experts were present: Dylan Wiliam, Paul Black, Mary James, Gordon Stobbard, Ruth Sutton and Richard Dougherty. The talks were challenging and inspiring and there was fervent discussion about the characteristics of 'Assessment for Learning' and 'Assessment as Learning' and the role of feedback. In 2018, Dylan summarised the insights from research on the effects of feedback in an Assessment-for-Learning approach in an interesting overview (Wiliam, 2018). Much of this research on effects is interesting, as long as we remember that the lion's share of that research has been conducted within the surpassed traditional 'knowledge transfer' paradigm and should therefore be interpreted in that way.

In the course of the past decades, many overview studies have been published on the effects of feedback. Already in the 1980s, several reviews appeared. Giving feedback was considered better than giving no feedback, but there were no clear results on how to maximise the benefits of feedback. Later, more studies and reviews appeared. One of the most well known is undoubtedly that of Avraham Kluger and Angelo DeNisi from 1996 in which they reported an overview of the research that was done between 1905 and 1995 into the effects of feedback. What do these studies show? How strong are the effects of feedback?

DOI: 10.4324/9781003294139-8

Review articles often use standardised effect sizes (Cohen, 1988) to indicate the extent of the impact. In the field of learning and development, these review articles can be found mainly in the Educational Research Review, the journal that Filip founded in 2000 to provide a platform for high-quality European review studies.

Kluger and DeNisi (1996) and Shute (2008) concluded in their review studies that the magnitude of the effect of feedback on pupil performance was between 0.4 and 0.8 standard deviations. Hattie and Timperley (2007) found on the basis of 74 meta-analyses comprising 4,157 primary studies that feedback increased pupils' performance by 0.94 standard deviations on average. According to Wiliam (2018), a weighting of 231 effect sizes (which have been published in previous research) in relation to sample size generated a mean effect of 0.41 standard deviations. According to Wiliam, this equates to more than a doubling of learners' learning speed. In their recent review, Wisniewski, Zierer and Hattie (2020) report an effect size of 0.48 and this was based on 994 effect sizes from 435 studies (61,000 subjects). If you assume that an effect size of 0.40 or higher is significant, then you can conclude from all these review studies that feedback really does matter. The effect found is sometimes so strong (as in the study of Hattie and Timperley) that it becomes almost implausible, according to Wiliam. So there is sufficient reason to say that feedback is a very powerful tool to increase the impact of learning.

Of course, sometimes feedback also has negative effects. This is mainly the case when feedback reduces the learner's autonomy or self-efficacy because feedback is controlling, negative or not informative at all. In any case, the more informative the feedback, the more effective it is (Wisniewski et al., 2020).

Even though most studies show clear positive effects, there are differences in the measured effect sizes. An explanation for these different results (and also sometimes very strong effects) certainly lies in the complexity of interpreting results from review studies. In the past, we developed a typology of feedback (Gielen, Dochy et al., 2011) in which we proposed to analyse feedback studies in terms of the many variables that play a role. When reading and interpreting the studies summarised in reviews, the use of this typology is useful for better understanding the type of feedback the reported effects are about.

Impactful feedback is dialogue

II

Where did the idea of feedback as dialogue come from?

From various angles, small and larger pieces of the puzzle of seeing feedback as a dialogue have been laid over the past decades. We discuss a number of them.

In addition to the effect sizes, the authors of a number of review studies also discuss the conditions under which feedback can have an effect. In the 1990s, Bangert-Drowns, Kulik, Kulik and Morgan (1991) and Kluger and DeNisi (1996) concluded that the crucial determinant of the effects of feedback was the extent to which the feedback was consciously understood by the recipient. This condition has also been pointed out in earlier reviews, for example Dempster (1991, 1992) and Elshout-Mohr (1994). Also more recently, many researchers stress that students find feedback difficult to understand and that teachers often find it difficult to explain what they mean (Blair & McGinty, 2013). Learners who do not understand the feedback due to, for example, the academic terminology used may not respond to the advice given (Chanock 2000; Maclellan 2001; Weaver 2006). Ivanic, Clark and Rimmershaw (2000) also argue that this failure to respond to feedback is partly due to students not understanding the 'expert' language of academic disciplines. As Nicol (2010) argues, if the 'input' message is unclear, the quality of student engagement with feedback is compromised, with feedback becoming a mere transfer of information. In particular, the study by Hattie and Timperley (2007) confirmed the earlier findings by Kluger and DeNisi (1996) that feedback that focuses on the processing of the task and on self-regulation of learning was usually more effective than person-centred feedback. A later review by Shute (2008) clarified that feedback is more effective when it provides some form of support on how to proceed, how to improve performance and thus when it encourages self-reflection on

DOI: 10.4324/9781003294139-10

next steps. In her recent review, Evans (2013) goes a step further. She agrees with the previously mentioned conditions but indicates that many of these conditions can only be realised when the learner is significantly involved in the feedback process, for example in developing their own action points after receiving feedback. She explicitly states that the feedback process is an honest dialogue between the learner and the coach (tutor) and any others to clarify meanings, expectations, misconceptions and future actions.

In summary, in the course of the past decades, authors of review studies discussed various conditions for effective feedback. To the question of how to realise these, the answer is by organising the feedback process as a dialogue.

In addition to the overview studies, more arguments for dialogue were found in studies of written feedback. A large proportion of the feedback given in education during the past decades and even today is still written, although it has already for a long time been known that written feedback is a very weak form. In extensive research into the quality of written feedback, Adalberon (2021) came up with the following results: the feedback is far too limited, rarely detailed, and teachers give general feedback that seems to be copied from the prescribed learning outcomes/criteria, and finally concepts such as 'relevant' and 'good' are highly open to interpretation. Written feedback has strong limitations, says Adalberon (2021). And writing feedback is not that simple: 'Writing understandable and useable feedback is a challenging task that requires systematic practice and builds on experience over time'. Adalberon concludes that: 'An approach like this … will probably result in a ritualised method for providing feedback that has limited value' (2021, p. 610). Blair and McGinty (2013) also showed that students are unhappy with feedback and that what they would really like is more verbal feedback, a more collaborative discussion between learners and coaches where learners are given the opportunity to develop their strengths and weaknesses. If written feedback has so many limitations, then how should it be done? O'Donovan, Rust and Price (2016) emphasise that oral feedback is more effective than written; face-to-face dialogue forces students to engage critically with their work and empowers them in their efforts to grow.

The next piece of argumentation for feedback dialogue is formed by research on the comparison between group tutorials and one-to-one tutorials. A study by Smith (2021) found that 89% of learners considered the latter the most useful feedback medium. In contrast, only 7% of participants found group tutorials the most useful feedback medium, and 24% found them the least useful. According to Smith (2021), learners have a strong preference for feedback dialogues because the discourse gives them a sense of agency. This learner agency affects in turn the learning impact. Other studies also confirmed these findings, namely students have a strong preference for continuous communication with a learning coach when it comes to feedback (Dowden, Pittaway, Yost, & McCarthy, 2013; Sutcliffe et al., 2019). Dowden and colleagues are extremely clear when they write: 'Ideally feedback is a continuing two-way communication that encourages progress'.

Another piece of the puzzle is formed by several scholars who emphasised that feedback is a cyclical process. Effective feedback is feedback that is heard, understood and accepted by the learner and thus helps to take further steps. In 2005, in his address when accepting the position of President of the European Association for Research on Learning, Filip stated the following:

> Feedback should be provided quickly enough to be useful to students and should be given both often enough and in enough detail. The quality of feedback is important. Feedback should focus on learning, be understandable for students and linked to the purpose of the tasks and the criteria. Students' response to feedback should be taken into consideration. Feedback should be received by and attended to the students and students should act upon the feedback in order to improve their tasks or their learning.
>
> (F. Dochy, EARLI presidential address, 2005)

In short, feedback is a cycle with the following steps:

1. Seeking/requesting feedback.
2. Sharing feedback in interaction/dialogue.
3. Understanding feedback.
4. Accepting feedback.
5. Turning feedback into action.

The key conditions for effective feedback indicating the importance of feedback as a dialogue are outlined in Box 7.1.

BOX 7.1

In summary: key conditions for effective feedback that indicate the importance of feedback as a dialogue

- Trust between the actors in the feedback process.
- Well understood feedback.

(Continued)

- Accepted feedback.
- Feedback that can be converted into an action plan, with follow-up by the learner and the coach. Feedback is particularly effective when it is followed up regularly and structurally.
- Cyclically and with great regularity.
- Narrative feedback more effective (possibly audio or video feedback) than written feedback.

Feedback as dialogue, what does it mean?

8

Where does the word dialogue come from and what does it mean? According to Isaacs (1994, p. 353), the word dialogue comes from Greek, where 'dia' means 'with each other' and 'logos' means 'the word'. On this basis, Isaacs (1994, p. 353) defines dialogue as 'the art of thinking together' and 'a sustained collective inquiry into everyday experience and what we take for granted'.

So what are feedback dialogues?

Feedback dialogues are frequent interactive exchanges between two or more parties in which opinions (about content, quality, etc.) based on concrete information are shared, interpretations are explained, meanings are exchanged and discussed and expectations are clarified in a climate of trust, of equality and of appropriate high expectations. They are an integral part of a learning process characterised by learner urgency, learner agency, collaboration and knowledge exchange. Each feedback dialogue consists of different steps (connection, feed-up, feedback, feedforward) mentioned in Box 8.1, whereby the feedforward is always the step for the next dialogue. The learner is at the wheel of the feedback dialogue. An important role of the coach is to facilitate the learner's navigation through the successive feedback dialogues.

We will address some crucial elements of a feedback dialogue.

DOI: 10.4324/9781003294139-11

BOX 8.1

Steps in feedback dialogue

1. Making a connection: being on the same wavelength (connection).
2. Feedback is requested, sought by the learner on the basis of the questions he/she has, the development goals he/she has (feed-up).
3. Feedback is registered by the learner (feedback).
4. Feedback is interpreted by the learner (feedback).
5. The learner accepts the feedback (feedback).
6. The learner summarises the feedback and transforms the feedback into a plan of action (feedforward).
7. The learner, coach and relevant others follow up the implementation of the action plan (feedforward) whereby the feedback cycle starts again.

Interactivity

First, the concept of feedback dialogue implies an **interactive element**. Black and Wiliam pointed this out in 2005: '… because the quality of interactive feedback is a critical feature in determining the quality of learning activity and is therefore a central feature of pedagogy' (Black & Wiliam, 2005, p. 100). Nicol and Macfarlane-Dick (2006) refer to feedback as a collaborative process that 'encourages teacher and peer dialogue around learning'. To emphasise the interactivity, Anseel and Brutus (2019) define feedback dialogue as a dyadic construct that involves interactions and exchange between two members of a dyad. According to the authors, both members of the dialogue are dependent on each other. The first aspect mentioned by the authors is relational dependence. Both feedback parties are dependent on each other in their interactions and must take this into account when engaging in the feedback process (Anseel et al., 2018). The authors argue that both dialogue members are receptive to each other's behaviour and feelings and change their behaviour accordingly in order to maintain or not maintain the relationship.

Behavioural reciprocity

A second relevant feature of feedback dialogue that is currently under-developed in the feedback literature is **behavioural reciprocity** (Anseel & Brutus, 2019). Most studies investigating the feedback-seeking process only focus on one member of the feedback dyad and are more concerned with how and why an employee might seek or give feedback rather than further exploring the interaction between the two parties. Behavioural reciprocity implies that there is a reciprocal interaction between the feedback seeker and feedback giver, in the sense that the feedback-giving behaviour is dependent on the feedback-seeking behaviour and vice versa. For example, a coach giving feedback that includes concrete tips to proceed will enhance feedback-seeking behaviour and feedback-seeking in a real curious way will enhance profound feedback. This reciprocity is also one of the essential elements in a dyadic relationship (Ferris et al., 2009). In one of the points below, we extend conceptualisation of Anseel and Brutus (2019) by arguing that more than two actors can be involved in a feedback dialogue (e.g. peers and/or externals).

Collaborative discussion

In addition, an element of feedback dialogue is **collaborative discussion**. Blair and McGinty (2013) defined 'feedback dialogue' as 'a collaborative discussion about feedback (between teacher and student or student and student) that enables shared understandings and then provides opportunities for further development based on the exchange'. We assume that this can take various forms, both face-to-face and electronically.

Learner agency

Dialogical feedback also implies '**learner agency**': the learner has an active role in asking for, seeking, generating feedback, recording it, interpreting it and linking an action plan to it. Nicol (2009) stated in this regard that 'students should be given a much more active and participatory role in assessment processes (p. 337)'. A suitable strategy for this is a conversation about an assignment and a feedback dialogue, in which the student can explain his ideas, ask questions, seek clarification and defend or explain his position.

Implementing feedback as a dialogue is often part of a particular approach to or vision of learning. According to Hill and West (2020), feedback must occupy a central position in a dialogical approach to learning. Feedback in dialogue contributes to the creation of meaning and understanding through discourse between the learner and learning coach. A feedback dialogue is therefore an integral part of a learning process in which knowledge is built up jointly in a collaborative process, with the learner taking the wheel (agency) and his/her questions and interests being the starting point (urgency).

Actors

Several actors are relevant in a feedback dialogue. The feedback dialogue does not only take place between the learner and coach. Peers are also an important source of feedback. The use of formative peer feedback (without asking students to assess each other's work) has shown that in many cases students are able to give effective feedback on each other's work (Falchikov, 2007). For this to work effectively, the learning environment must of course be supportive. For example, learners need to feel comfortable and trust each other, and this is best achieved by developing peer-learning communities that are not based on hierarchy.

Feedback landscape: two-way; equality; power balance

A feedback dialogue takes place in equality. The metaphors that students used in Blair and McGinty's (2013) study, such as 'running after feedback', 'chasing' and 'chasing' teachers, indicate how in some cases obtaining oral feedback required a high degree of tenacity and determination from students where they are in a subordinate position. Feedback as dialogue means a two-way exchange, a discussion, and leads to a balance of power on a more equal footing. Evans (2013) speaks in this context of a feedback landscape that is changing. Actors in a feedback landscape must take into account dimensions such as awareness, power, community, process and resources. The process of feedback exchange and the use of tools depends on factors such as awareness, power and community, which in turn are influenced by the outcomes of the process as part of an iterative cycle of conversations. According to Evans (2013), the effectiveness of feedback depends largely on the Assessment-as-Learning design, which can enhance or limit learners' agency in the feedback process.

The feedback landscape illustrates a two-way process that highlights the relationship between learner and coach but also recognises that this is not the main or only source of feedback exchange. As indicated in the previous section, other sources such as peers, other experts or coaches, the internet and so on are also part of the feedback landscape. Evans' feedback landscape relies on feedback exchange to emphasise the continuous and iterative nature of the process (Evans, 2013):

1. A key role of the coach is to facilitate the learner's navigation through the landscape.
2. Coaches and learners can both act as givers and receivers of feedback.
3. Coaches and learners are part of different learning communities outside of the direct relationship between the giver and receiver of feedback.
4. The coach is not the only or primary source of feedback, but often the most used and valued source.
5. The feedback landscape offers opportunities and barriers to learning; learner agency is important.
6. Individuals will experience barriers and opportunities differently.
7. A large number of exchanges take place within complex networks in which decision-making and filtering take place on the basis of the value of sources and the content of feedback.
8. Feedback exchanges between individuals are based on previous learning experiences and a shared understanding of what is good.
9. Feedback exchanges differ due to individual learning differences and due to differences in context.
10. Awareness of subject/domain-specific knowledge and communication skills is important in feedback exchanges.
11. Social interaction does not always require the physical presence of others.
12. Learners can learn by observing the feedback exchanges of others without necessarily seeking them out themselves.

Earlier in this book, we used the concepts of connection, feed-up, feed-back and feedforward as the steps in the cyclical process of feedback.

Sustainable feedback

The feedback dialogue focuses not only on performance or learning outcomes but also, and especially, on the learning process. Only then is feedback, as Carless and colleagues (2011) call it, sustainable. The feedback dialogue is the carrier of the cyclical feedback process. In order to achieve impactful learning, immediate and specific feedback on task performance that is aimed at improvement through a cyclical process is essential. In this context, Carless et al. (2011, p. 397) speak of sustainable feedback as: 'dialogic processes and activities which can support and inform the student on the current task, whilst also developing the ability to self-regulate performance on future tasks'.

Training within the old transfer paradigm focused primarily on performance and not on learning. Wiliam (2018) gave a clear argument why performance does not equal learning. One can learn even if there is no performance improvement (Soderström & Bjork, 2015). An improvement in performance can also occur without an increase in long-term learning, and an improvement in performance on a specific task can also be accompanied by a decrease in long-term learning. Because students base their assessment of their own learning on performance improvement (rather than long-term learning), they tend to use study strategies that improve short-term performance rather than long-term learning. Everyone has experienced that memorising often leads to good performance (which is why we keep repeating this successful strategy) and also that we forget most of what we have memorised very quickly (Dochy, Segers, & Dochy, 2020).

These insights also partly explain the contradictory findings on feedback interventions. Feedback can seem effective in the short term by improving performance but have no effect on long-term learning. Conversely, feedback can appear to be completely ineffective (no performance improvement) but can, over time, trigger a learning process that leads to long-term learning and even higher performance levels (Wiliam, 2018).

The characteristics of 'feedback in dialogue' is summarised in Box 8.2.

BOX 8.2

In summary: What are the characteristics of 'feedback in dialogue'?

- Interaction between relevant actors (students, coaches, peers, relevant external actors).
- Creating meaning and understanding through discourse between participants in the feedback dialogue.
- Dealing with learning outcomes and learning process. A process-oriented feedback dialogue is more sustainable than a performance-oriented feedback dialogue.
- Learner agency.
- Part of a vision of learning where agency, urgency and collaboration are central.
- A feedback landscape with equality between the actors in the feedback exchange.
- The bearer of a cyclical process (sustainable feedback).

Characteristics of a feedback dialogue that stimulates learning

9

Steen-Utheim and Wittek (2017) built a model of feedback dialogue and related learning opportunities, although they themselves also indicate that their research still took place in a more traditional setting of unbalanced dialogue and transmission. Their model of dialogic feedback (2017) points to a number of core aspects that stimulate opportunities for learning. An impactful feedback dialogue looks like this:

1. Emotional and relational support: Emotions influence active participation and engagement. Creating a safe learning environment, ensuring empathy and trust, addressing on a first name basis, acknowledging learners' emotional responses and so on lead to increased learning opportunities and learning from feedback.
2. Maintain dialogue: Dialogue is the essence of thought and language and shapes cognitive development. Encouraging dialogue supports growth and development through knowledge sharing with peers. Learning is fostered by starting a new discussion and using a dynamic question and answer format.
3. Expressing oneself: Have learners ask questions that cause them to reflect on their understanding and misunderstandings, that is, meta-questions, in order to achieve active feedback dialogue.
4. Having peers contributes to individual growth: The support of a competent other creates opportunities for the exchange of one's own experiences, of feedback, for individual cognitive development. Challenge learners to ask questions that lead to reflection and self-expression.

DOI: 10.4324/9781003294139-12

In line with point 1 of Steen-Utheim and Wittek's model of dialogical feedback, Losada and Heaphy (2004) point out that feedback has an effect on emotion and, conversely, emotion also has an effect on the learning process. They define positive feedback as feedback that shows support, encouragement or appreciation, and negative feedback as feedback that shows disapproval. Their research, which analysed verbal communication between members of 60 management teams, showed that a high ratio of positive-to-negative feedback was a crucial factor in high-performing teams and that low ratios were characteristic of low-performing teams (Voerman, Meijer, Korthagen, & Simons, 2014). They state: 'Positivity and negativity interact as powerful feedback systems to generate different emotional spaces' (Losada & Heaphy, 2004, p. 744). In that regard, they found that positive and negative feedback create emotional spaces. Positive feedback creates expansive emotional spaces that open up opportunities for learning. Negative feedback, on the other hand, creates restricted emotional spaces that close off learning (see also similar findings in Voerman et al., 2014). Earlier, Fredrickson (2001) also described similar findings on the constricting influence of negative emotions on a person's momentary thinking and acting repertoire (Losada & Heaphy, 2004).

In line with point 3 of Steen-Utheim and Wittek's model (2017), learning coaches play a role in supporting learners in developing a proactive mindset. This means helping learners discover what it means concretely to be active participants in the feedback process and to make a step-by-step plan based on feedforward. The review by Thurlings, Vermeulen, Bastiaens and Stijnen (2013) also emphasised this element: effective feedback is enhanced in the context of coaching, peer-coaching or intervision (i.e. coaches supporting and coaching each other). In this way, the feedback dialogue can help develop not only self-efficacy (the belief that you can realise your plans (Van Dinther, Dochy, & Segers, 2011)) but also self-regulation (the ability to plan, monitor and evaluate your progress and to think strategically about it) (Hill & West, 2020).

The above is consistent with the way David Carless conceptualised feedback dialogues in 2006, namely as a dynamic interaction between three dimensions: the cognitive dimension (asking for explanations; explaining a view; describing or questioning insights; explaining progress), the socio-affective dimension (expressing empathy; expressing doubts or certainties) and the structural dimension (cyclical planning of the dialogues; following up the feedback reports; checking the approach to the feedforward). In 2011, Carless, Salter, Yang and Lam (2011, p. 397) added the element of sustainability and defined sustainable feedback as 'dialogical processes and activities that support the learner in his/her task and also develop the ability

> **BOX 9.1**
>
> *Characteristics of dialogical feedback with impact*
>
> - Cognitive dimension: Sharing knowledge with peers and externals, new discussion, dynamic questions and answers, asking for explanations, explaining a vision, describing or questioning insights, explaining progress, expressing oneself, presenting progress/intermediate products, stimulating reflection and expressing oneself.
> - Emotional dimension: Ensuring empathy and trust, addressing learners on a first name basis, acknowledging emotional reactions of learners and expressing doubts or certainties. A lot of positive feedback leads to emotional space for learning.
> - Structural dimension: Cyclical (weekly/bi-weekly) planning of dialogues; connection, feed-up, feedback, feedforward; following up the feedback reports; checking the approach of the feedforward/action plan.

to self-regulate performance on future tasks'. Dialogic feedback fits with 'future learning' because it encourages 'learner agency' (stronger engagement, see Price, Handley, & Millar, 2011, and self-regulation of learning, see Winstone, Nash, Parker, & Rowntree, 2017). Also Dai Hounsell already pointed out the aspect of sustainability of feedback in 2007: Feedback is effective when the impact extends beyond the task to which the feedback relates; there is congruence between coaching and feedback through a productive dialogue in which the student plays an active role in generating, interpreting and putting the feedback to concrete use (see also Box. 9.1 for the overview of the characteristics of dialogical feedback with impact).

How often should we have feedback dialogues?

Within the concept of high-impact learning, the learner is given a strong degree of 'learner agency' and actually determines the rhythm of the feedback dialogues. Many High Impact Learning that Lasts (HILL)-based training programmes encourage learners to have weekly or bi-weekly feedback dialogues (both for the individual learner and for the teams). Then, dialogues are experienced as cyclical and learners have fresh memories of their actions and performances. For experienced and autonomous learners, the feedback dialogues may be slightly further apart.

Are feedback dialogues always focused on the learning process and the learning outcomes of the individual learner?

Learning with impact means that we often work in teams. We take on challenges that we sometimes tackle individually, but much more often we do so in teams. Do team feedback dialogues replace individual feedback dialogues? The answer is clear: no. Understanding feedback, the emotions associated with feedback and the individual step-by-step plans that learners make remain personal matters. Learners need team feedback and personal feedback and need it to monitor their own development.

Do we end up with even more feedback dialogues? More frequent than weekly? No

We end up looking for a balance between individual feedback dialogues and team feedback dialogues. With experienced learners in a HILL-based training, the balance will be created by the learners themselves. After all, they themselves request their feedback dialogues. With starters, we as trainers will make a proposal and evaluate after some time whether adjustments are needed.

Can we conceptualise team feedback in the same way as individual feedback? No. How individual team members deal with feedback and what they do with it influences how the team deals with team feedback and vice versa (London and Sessa, 2006). Therefore, it makes sense to distinguish the feedback dialogue at the team level from that at the individual level. We will discuss the team feedback dialogue in a separate section below.

The team feedback dialogue   **10**

Gabelica and Popov (2020, p. 255) define feedback in team settings as 'the transmission of information to team members or the team as a whole about actions, events, processes, or behaviours relative to task completion or teamwork'. They describe team feedback as an important way of regulating teamwork. This is done by discussing team processes and team deliverables, for example, discussing with the team when it is in danger of straying from the goal or the predetermined plan, stimulating the team to reflect on this and take action. It is noteworthy that Gabelica and Popov (2020) talk about passing on information (one-way traffic from the coach) and not about sharing and discussing information with each other (dialogue). Yet they indicate that changes in team processes and team performance will only take place when, during the feedback moments, the team collectively discusses the feedback, interprets it and jointly enters into a conversation about how to convert the feedback into follow-up actions. Herewith they implicitly refer to the importance of the feedback dialogue. Jabri (2004, p. 141) also stresses the importance of what he calls 'to dialogize differences in perceptions'. He states that learning from feedback occurs optimally when team members discuss with each other how they interpret the feedback and their differences in interpretations and together give meaning to them. They formulate this as follows: 'Rather than averaging perceptions, which purports to represent the group, it is of benefit to use individual differences in perceptions to advance members' construction of their situation and to act as a springboard for them to learn from the feedback itself' (p. 141).

We go one step further. Dialogue is essential in every step of the feedback process, during the connection, the feed-up, the feedback and the

DOI: 10.4324/9781003294139-13

Group Situation & Characteristics

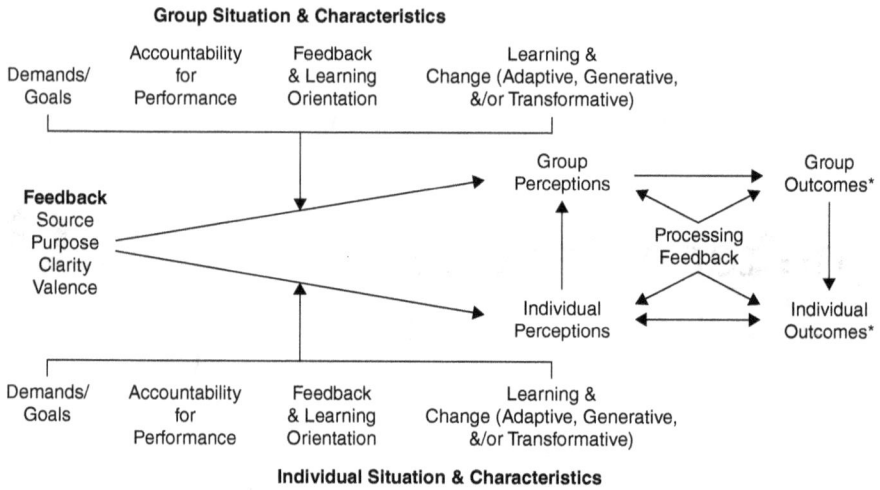

Figure 10.1 The Team Feedback Model (free after London and Sessa, 2006).

feedforward; during the formulation of the feedback question up to and including the conversion of the generated feedback into follow-up actions.

London and Sessa described the process of team feedback in 2006. Their description of the team feedback process is shown in Figure 10.1. The model indicates that the characteristics of feedback influence the perceptions of feedback of both the individual team member and the team as a whole. The characteristics of feedback are the source, namely where does the feedback information come from (personal source such as supervisor or colleague or information such as a grade, time spent and whether it is experienced as objective or subjective), the function of the feedback, namely formative or summative, the clarity and the sign namely positive or negative feedback. These characteristics of feedback have been discussed earlier.

In addition, individual and group characteristics influence how individuals and teams perceive feedback. These characteristics of team and individual are the goals that individual and group set for themselves (or challenges they face), the sense of responsibility they have for functioning well and for learning from mistakes, their learning or performance orientation (feedback and learning orientation) and how individual and team learn, namely adaptive (reactive learning), generative (proactive learning) or transformative (learning aimed at radical changes in perspectives). How the individual team member and the team as a whole perceive the feedback is related to each other and mutually influences each other. Both have an impact on how the individual and the team deal with feedback. This in turn has an impact on the returns to the team and to each individual team member.

In addition to Gabelica and Popov (2020) and the model of London and Sessa (2006), we agree with Jabri (2004) that the team feedback dialogue plays an important role in clarifying how individual team members experience and interpret feedback. Discussing this with each other helps the individual and the team to get a better understanding of what the feedback means. This helps the individual and the team to better deal with the feedback, to achieve depth in the content, to transform the feedback into an action plan, into learning activities that contribute to optimising learning gains for the individual and the team.

Power relationships

11

In order to understand feedback and feedback dialogues, it is also good to take a closer look at power and power relations. Power relations in particular can play a very stimulating or destructive role in feedback dialogues.

The extent to which previous feedback contributions were valued can influence learners' willingness and ability to engage in feedback dialogue. For the coach, it is about the extent to which choices and ownership are encouraged for learners within a low-power difference relationship. In addition to the quality of the relationship between the two parties, the broader environment in which the feedback dialogue takes place also has a significant impact on the feedback exchange (Ashford, De Stobbeleir, & Nujella, 2016). One of these contextual antecedents that research has primarily focused on is the relationship between the requester and giver. Anseel and Brutus (2019) have called this relational dependency and formulated it as a second feedback dialogue characteristic. We briefly discuss the quality of the two main relationship types, namely the supervisor/coach-subordinate relationship and the relationship between peers or equals and how they influence interactions within feedback dialogue.

Coach/supervisor-subordinate relationship (LMX)

The most widely accepted relationship theory regarding the quality of the coach/supervisor-subordinate relationship is the leader-member exchange (LMX) theory, which was summarised in Box 11.1 by Graen and Scandura (1987). The LMX theory assumes that coaches have a unique

DOI: 10.4324/9781003294139-14

BOX 11.1

Coach-learning relationship (LMX)

- Coaches have a unique relationship with each of their learners.
- A high-quality relationship includes mutual trust, positive affection, loyalty, respect and a willingness to go beyond simple agreements or expectations (low-power distance).
- High-quality relationships give rise to more feedback-seeking behaviour from the coach and more frequent feedback-seeking behaviour.
- Coaches who are unsupportive and punitive in their response to poor performance create a negative environment in which future feedback dialogues are more likely to be avoided.

---

relationship with each of their subordinates (Graen & Uhl-Bien, 1995). High-quality LMX includes mutual trust, positive affection, loyalty, respect and a willingness to go beyond simple agreements or expectations (low-power distance). Low-quality LMX, on the other hand, can be characterised as a lack of mutual trust, respect, loyalty and unwilling-ness to go beyond expectations, often seen in high power distance (Moss, Sanchez, Brumbaugh, & Borkowski, 2009).

A consistent finding in the LMX research is that high-quality relationships are related to feedback-seeking behaviour. Research has shown that coach/supervisor support and trust, mutual communication and respect are posi-tively related to feedback seeking. Together, these findings suggest that the relationship between high-quality LMX and feedback-seeking behaviour is robust (Ashford et al., 2016). There is also growing evidence suggesting that poor LMX is related to reduced feedback-seeking behaviour and more related to feedback avoidance behaviour (Moss et al., 2009). Research shows that coaches who respond unsupportively and punitively to poor perform-ance create a negative environment in which people are more likely to avoid future feedback dialogues with them.

With regard to feedback-seeking patterns, Chen, Lam and Zhong (2007) found that high-quality LMX gives rise to more feedback seeking by the coach or supervisor and to more frequent feedback-seeking behaviour. Individuals in high-quality LMX are more likely to use direct strategies than indirect methods (e.g. monitoring). LMX also influences the motives behind seeking feedback.

Relationship between equals or peers

'Equivalent status relationships' are relationships between peers who have no formal authority over each other (Sias, Krone, & Jablin, 2002). Since learners typically have only one or a few coaches/leaders but many peers/colleagues, it is essential to note that these types of relationships represent the bulk of relationships. Peer relationships vary equally in their quality. Kram and Isabella (1985) constructed a comprehensive system for categorising peer relationships in which they distinguished three primary types: (1) informative peer relationships, (2) collegial peer relationships and (3) special peer relationships (see Box 11.2).

Informative peer relationships are characterised by a low level of trust and personal involvement and openness. In this relationship, the exchange of work-related information is most useful for the peers. As a result of these characteristics, peers are less likely to receive any emotional support or affirmation (Kram & Isabella, 1985). Interestingly, Kram and Isabella (1985) found that the 'information peer relationship' is the most common in organisations. Due to the instrumental focus of this relationship (i.e. providing information about projects/assignments/work) and the low level of trust, it is to be expected that individuals engage in very limited feedback exchanges, focusing only on project-related topics.

The second relationship between peers, **the collegial peer relationship**, is characterised by a moderate level of trust and personal involvement and openness (Kram & Isabella, 1985). In contrast to the informational peer relationship, this relationship type offers not only more extensive information exchange (i.e. broader content, including both project-related information and limited personal topics) but also higher levels of emotional support, work-related feedback and affirmation. Peers in this relationship type tend to be mostly collaborative. Because of the moderate levels of trust and support, the collegial peer relationship provides significant amounts of project-related feedback. Moreover, Sias (2015) found that the quality of information provided in this relationship is the highest of the three relationship types.

Finally, **the special peer relationship** offers high levels of mutual trust and personal involvement and openness due to its almost unlimited communication breadth with much exchange of information on personal and project-related topics (Kram & Isabella, 1985; Sias, 2015). Individuals in such relationships find a lot of emotional support, affirmation and there is a great emotional bond between the peers. Kram and Isabella (1985) suggested that this type of relationship is rare and needs several years to develop. Because of the high degree of trust, openness and safety, professionals in

---

BOX 11.2

Power and relationships in feedback dialogue

- Relational dependency plays a significant role in feedback dialogue.
- Two main types of relationships play a role, namely the relationship between supervisor and subordinate, also referred to as leader-member ex-change (LMX), and the relationship between peers of the same level.
- While high-quality LMX is positively related to seeking feedback and using direct search methods, low-quality LMX is associated with feedback avoidance behaviour.
- Regarding the collegial working relationship, there are three forms of relationship with different levels of trust and personal involvement and openness, namely informative, collegial and special peer relationships. The collegial peer (i.e. a moderate level of trust and self-disclosure) is related to the highest quality of information received.

---

such relationships engage in an exchange of personal feedback. However, contrary to expectations, Sias (2015) showed that special peer relationships were not related to high information quality.

How individuals see their role(s) within the feedback dialogue is crucial. Poulos and Mahony (2008) pointed out that the transference model was still too much in favour and as a result students were seen as passive partners in the feedback process for too long. Hattie and Timperley (2007) found that too much attention has been paid to what the teacher can do to provide effective feedback and what the learner should do to make more use of the feedback provided, and that students too often see feedback as the responsibility of the course. A truly collaborative model of feedback as dialogue was not within reach at the time. Implementing a collaborative feedback design means that all parties must see feedback as an integral iterative element of the learning process and not as an add-on (Miller, Doering, & Scharber, 2010).

Learners in the study by Blair and McGinty (2013) valued opportunities for dialogue with teachers. Yet that study also revealed an unbalanced power relationship with the teacher as the 'expert' giving the student very little control over their own learning. High-impact learning requires a 'deeper' dialogue with a balanced power relationship, more ownership and responsibility for learners. Feedback dialogues, according to Blair and McGinty, need to take on more of a conversation character, a two-way exchange, a discussion. Using the term conversation or discussion shifts the balance of power and places learner and coach on a more equal footing. Feedback dialogues should therefore be more collaborative, with partnership, which also facilitates student interaction and knowledge sharing, where feedback is also exchanged frequently, cyclically, in between (after discussions, draft assignments, intermediate products, etc.).

A balanced power relationship means that the learning coach has a mindset characterised by a desire to continually learn about learners' learning and to use this information to make decisions (Fluckiger et al., 2010). A mindset of accurately diagnosing and dialoguing about the appropriate support to be provided. A mindset of coaching as supporting the learning process and wanting to take into account the level of learners, their ability to use advice and their emotional responses to feedback. Coaches need training and support to do this.

Learners need a mindset of being responsible for their own learning, of being active in the feedback process, of seeking feedback themselves and sharing their interpretation of the feedback, and of being prepared to continually self-reflect. But they also need support.

This mindset on the part of the coach and the learner is a prerequisite for the short-term emergence of a shared understanding of quality, which is crucial if the feedback process is to lead effectively to learning gains.

The feedback dialogue in practice   **12**

In the first instance, we will ensure that feedback discussions take place with high regularity. That means weekly at the start. If we are in a training programme where there is a 'high-impact learning' mode or a strong learning climate, learners will very quickly get into the habit of arranging a weekly meeting with the learning coach themselves. It is then sufficient for the learning coach to communicate what is expected to be weekly feedback dialogues. Within a few months, a good feedback culture can already develop in which a feedback dialogue is experienced by learners as something nice, a tool, a privilege, something convenient and useful and so on. If that does not happen so quickly, then it is mainly a matter of continuing to do it, unless there are signals from students that they are not looking forward to it, do not attach much importance to it or do not see any use in it. Then, there is something wrong in the design of the feedback dialogues. In the case of pre-arranged feedback dialogues, it is best to keep the following list in Table 12.1 in mind, but it is also worth keeping it in mind for spontaneous feedback discussions.

DOI: 10.4324/9781003294139-15

Table 12.1 Tips for the coach for an effective feedback dialogue

Tips for a coach

1. Meet at a suitable place
   - Always arrange for a feedback dialogue as soon as possible after a completed learning activity or as soon as the learner feels it is necessary
   - Any space where you feel comfortable is fine: a separate room, a corner in a learning hub, an online room, a spot in the coffee area, etc.
   - Find a more private place if the other person is uncomfortable getting a lot of attention
   - Allow enough time so that you are not rushed
   - Never give only
   - Sleep on it sometimes if you are upset or stressed; letting it sink in leads to more balanced feedback
2. Give feedback in person
   - Face-to-face (offline or online) feedback dialogues are 'two-way street' (rather than feedback in an email, in a paper, etc.). This gives both people more chance to understand exactly what it is about and to ask for further clarification
   - Be aware of your body language. Smile when it is appropriate and listen by turning your body towards the other person and nodding to show that you understand them
3. Prepare yourself
   - Ask yourself what you want to achieve with the conversation
   - Ask the learner what he wants to discuss. What is going well and what is more difficult. Plan what you want to talk about and what you want to say
   - Be specific and use examples, ask questions to elicit the views and ideas of the other and encourage a two-way conversation – e.g. how did you think it went? What could we have done differently?
   - Start with an open mind and expect new information
   - Think about how the other would prefer to receive feedback and focus on that
4. During a feedback dialogue
   - Ask first about their day/weekend/family before you start giving feedback if you know that this will make the other person feel more at ease. So always make a good connection first
   - Start the conversation by first asking the learner's view of the past week: How did it go? How did it feel? Are you satisfied? What went well (and what not)? Why? So first encourage self-feedback
   - Encourage a two-way conversation by asking questions and listening (the learner should do most of the talking)
   - Give specific feedback and give examples. Give two/three constructive feedbacks. Express negative feedback in the form of a question
   - Determine together what action needs to be taken. Have the learner list an action plan

(Continued)

Table 12.1 Tips for the coach for an effective feedback dialogue *(Continued)*

Tips for a coach

- Take a time-out: If the conversation starts to get emotional or you need time to 'process' what is being said – take a break
- Check if the other person has understood what you said. Have the learner repeat the step-by-step plan (based on the feedforward) in conclusion
- Agree who reports on the feedback session and how
- Keep your feedback very focused if you know the other person prefers to get straight to the point

5. After the feedback dialogue
    - Since feedback dialogues are always conversations about performance and development, agree that the learner makes a report (possibly in a predetermined template) of what was discussed
    - Check the report, approve it, add to it or give an overall assessment (smiley face, neutral face, sad face). In this way, the report becomes a shared reflection of the conversation, just as the feedback dialogue is a mutual process
    - Remember that the learner may need some time to reflect on what was discussed in the feedback dialogue – they may come to you later with questions or comments
    - Make sure that you do all the actions that you have committed to do, e.g. I will email you a case study, a paper from another organisation, a template, etc.
    - In the next feedback dialogue, go back to the action plan and the working points discussed. Follow this up or, better still, encourage the learner to do so

Barriers to impactful feedback dialogue

13

Yang and Carless's (2013) analysis reveals three different levels of barriers to dialogic feedback: institution-related barriers, the grade culture and learner-related barriers as mentioned in Box 13.1.

One of the main institution-related barriers to dialogic feedback is the modularised structure in training courses (Carless, Salter, Yang, & Lam, 2011; Jonsson, 2013; Yang & Carless, 2013). Yang and Carless (2013) found that an assignment divided into two or more phases makes iterative feedback cycles more possible, improving engagement with feedback and prospects for improvement from one subtask to another.

In his research, Taras (2006) showed that only 5 out of 166 modules allowed for an iterative feedback cycle. Students then receive feedback at the very end of (or even after) the course, which means that there are no opportunities to really apply their feedback in that learning process. Feedback in these situations is often perceived as irrelevant by learners (Winstone et al., 2017). Learning units that focus on high-impact learning therefore often comprise 15 credits and usually 30 credits. In such learning units that run longer times, feedback can be used to work with, to increase quality of output and so that cyclical feedback dialogues are seen as truly stimulating and can serve as the backbone of learning.

A second barrier has to do with whether the feedback is accompanied by a judgment expressed in terms of scores or grades. According to Winstone et al. (2016), students often focus heavily on grades at the expense of their engagement with qualitative feedback. Learners value grades, especially when they are accompanied by a lot of explanation (Ferguson, 2011; Walker, 2009). However, grades are especially problematic according to many

DOI: 10.4324/9781003294139-16

BOX 13.1

Obstacles to an impactful feedback dialogue

- Institution-related obstacles
  - A modularised structure in training
    - Solution: a task divided into two or more phases makes it more possible to have iterative feedback
- The number culture as an obstacle
  - Feedback that is accompanied by a grade
    - Solution: strengths and weaknesses for the criteria named in the rubrics are the input for the feedback dialogue
- Learner's barriers
  - No trust in the guidance and no active role in the feedback dialogue
    - Solution: ensure connection and trust; give many choices to the learner
- Contextual barriers
  - No feedback culture
    - Solution: create a clear, shared vision of feedback dialogues in the team; see feedback as a co-constructive process in order to create a respectful relationship between individuals, between learner and learning partner/coach.

---

researchers (Panadero & Jonsson, 2013). Grades mainly cause learners to do their best to comply with the teacher's comments, even if this means putting aside their own goals or interests (Zhao, 2010). Worse, if the effort of complying with the comments is perceived as too heavy, learners will make only those changes that pay off in terms of grades (McDowell, 2008). Such strategies mainly lead to superficial revisions (Panadero & Jonsson, 2013). Grades also have a detrimental effect on learners' self-esteem; they are discouraged and also ensure that students with good grades do not read their feedback for satisfaction. Lipnevich and Smith (2009) found that detailed descriptive feedback was most effective when given without a grade.

Grades can be seen as a potential barrier for improvement / development and, according to research, are the biggest obstacles for the productive use of feedback. Panadero and Jonsson (2020) conclude on the basis of a systematic literature review that the use of rubrics (for more information on rubrics, see Chapter 3, p. 37) for formative purposes should best not include quantifiable performance levels. Rubrics that support a feedback dialogue contain qualitative information and not quantitative information (grades). Grades are not meaningful input for the feedback dialogue; the strengths and the working points for the criteria named in the rubric are the input for the feedback dialogue.

A third barrier lies with the learner. 'Urgency', namely having a real need for feedback, and 'learner agency', namely having an active role in the feedback dialogue, play an important role. In addition, the confidence of the learner in the guidance in understanding and using feedback is essential for an effective feedback process (Panadero and Jonsson, 2020). When learners have the confidence in the coach, and in the process, they are motivated to take an active role in the feedback process and truly use the feedback to optimise the learning process and learning outcomes, feedback dialogues will generate full impact.

We add a fourth barrier to dialogic feedback: the context of the feedback dialogue. Feedback dialogue needs an appropriate context to be successful. That means a course in which there is a shared vision of learning and, as part of that, of feedback. The HILL model shows the different building blocks that together create impactful learning, where feedback as a dialogue is one component. Testimonies from higher and secondary education students have shown us that in a programme with high-impact learning as a scientific basis, a kind of 'mindset' quickly develops that facilitates the feedback dialogues: learners take more responsibility, feel better about themselves, do not show up with fear, dare to set their own challenges, dare to push their limits, see their own development more and enjoy it, let people know that they want more. There is no miracle recipe to get there in terms of to-do's for every day of the week. Practice shows that training programmes that strive to build that mindset as a team through a shared vision also get there. After all, all theories on change management also indicate that 'shared vision' is the first and necessary step for sustainable innovation.

Feedback dialogues fit within training programmes where, in addition to a mindset that facilitates feedback dialogues, there is a feedback culture. A feedback culture has a fragile relationship with leadership. Power and insecurity go hand in hand. The strong reduction of power relationships is necessary to create a climate of safety, respect and the ability to open up in order to learn (for more information on power and relationships, see Chapter 11). Respect and trust are also two sides of the same coin. Learners only achieve truly profound learning in a psychologically safe environment but an intensive feedback culture also requires dialogue in a safe environment.

A feedback culture is contagious, just like a power culture. A CEO with strong directive and authoritarian behaviour will give rise to identical behaviour among middle management, which in turn will make a learning culture and a feedback culture impossible. The creation of a feedback culture will be strongly facilitated by a leadership that asks feedback questions, seeks feedback, asks for advice, is open to learning and is in constant dialogue.

Dialogues can be fostered by promoting respect in the feedback and by avoiding signals of disrespect to create a safe environment (Zhou, Dawson, Tai, & Bearman, 2021). Two review articles (Panadero, 2016; van Gennip, Segers, & Tillema, 2009) have previously examined factors related to the interpersonal aspects of peer feedback, such as emotions, discomfort, psychological safety and group commitment to values and so on.

If we conceive of feedback as a co-constructive process, a respectful relationship between individuals becomes essential to sustain the interactions and achieve mutual growth, according to Zhou et al. (2021). A mutually respectful relationship involves not only peers but also working with an 'authority' who is experienced, has certain expertise and can think on the meta-level. A feedback dialogue is impactful when this authority is accepted as a learning partner, as a discussion partner in the connection, feed-up, feedback and feedforward and thus as a learning coach.

Feedback dialogue as the core of effective PCP coaching

14

Every book on coaching also deals with feedback. Feedback is in fact the core of effective coaching, but of course, there are various forms of coaching and also various goals that can be achieved through coaching, for example, coaching to change your own behaviour, coaching to exercise better, coaching to lose weight and coaching to learn.

Almost all forms of coaching are based on feedback. Coaching for learning is no different, but we can use various forms of feedback to shape the coaching. As far as we are concerned, this also ties in with the principles of power-oriented coaching (Korthagen & Nuijten, 2020): tapping into the power of the learner's strengths, teaching the learner to become autonomous and self-directing, and creating depth by embedding in authentic contact. Within that framework, coaching learning projects, for example, both content- and process-oriented coaching, will be necessary at the team level as well as the individual level. Also, it is good to coach in a monitoring way so that there is a good progress/development and a strong depth.

We stick to a clear concept as PCP coaching: progress, content and process (PCP) coaching. The PCP in this process is the learner. We start from that perspective, not from so-called right answers and corrective feedback.

PCP coaching offers a helping hand to every learning coach to keep focusing on the core elements of coaching: aiming for progress or growth (P), deepening and understanding the content (C) and reaching an optimal work process (P). These three aspects run continuously in a dialogue in which connection is continuously strengthened. And this is partly achieved by sharing feed-up, feedback and feedforward.

DOI: 10.4324/9781003294139-17

Coaching: content-oriented and process-oriented feedback – how do you get to the content?

A learning coach enters into a feedback dialogue and knows how to maintain a good partnership with the learner. The feedback on the agenda is balanced between content-oriented feedback and process-oriented feedback. Content-oriented feedback concerns quality aspects of the content of the learning activity (task, assignment, project challenge). Process-oriented feedback focuses on facilitating the learning process in order to successfully complete the learning activity. Process-oriented coaching is thus reflecting together on steps taken in the individual process and in the team process.

Table 14.1 contains sample questions that can guide the process-oriented feedback dialogue between coach and learners.

Table 14.1 Example questions for the process-oriented feedback dialogue between coach and learners

Process-oriented coaching of the individual learner:
• How are you doing with your subtask?
• Where do you stand? When will it be completed?
• How do you feel?
• What would you describe as a top moment?
• What motivates you to continue like this?
• What went well? Where did it go difficult?
• How do you deal with such a problem?
• Why do you deal with it in this way?
• How do you want to tackle it?
• Do you need anything else to deal with it quickly?

Process-oriented coaching of teams:
• How is the cooperation going?
• Is it efficient to work with each other?
• How do you experience the cooperation?
• How do you deal with setbacks?
• How do you motivate yourself to continue?
• What are top moments in the teamwork?
• How do you make teamwork a pleasant experience?
• What could be better? What would you like to change and why?
• How are we going to do that?
• What do we expect for next week?
• Who will take on what?

Content-oriented coaching provides depth and understanding. Content-oriented coaching is done by asking in-depth and understanding questions, solution-oriented questions, application in new situations, analysis, summarising/synthesising, explaining/clarifying and schematising and this also at the individual and team level. Hence, the rule applies: use whiteboards as much as possible! And let learners continuously question each other and add questions as a coach. In this way, as a coach, you fulfil a model function for asking constructively critical questions. Examples of questions are (when learner are doing a project on using water turbines for example): Can you sketch that dynamics model of a turbine? What are the real differences between types of water turbines? Can you draw those differences? Sketch your project timeline please? Summarise that on the whiteboard?.

The more often you as a learning coach ask to sketch these questions on a whiteboard, the more learners will prepare themselves and the more depth the meetings will gain. Make sure it is as non-threatening as possible, let others add to it, and let them build something as a team, that is, co-construct, add to it themselves and so on.

Do yourself as a coach a favour: ask several learners at each meeting to explain content to others on the whiteboard; after a few weeks, everyone will show up well prepared. Table 14.2 provides examples of content-oriented learning activities that the coach encourages the learners to engage in.

Table 14.2 Examples of content-oriented learning activities the coach encourages the learners to engage in

A learning coach continuously encourages the learners (individual, team) to:
• summarise
• outline on the whiteboard/smartboard
• outline the solution route
• outline the plan of approach
• also summarise this
• everyone reflects on this
• summarise this again on the whiteboard
• express their own vision on a subject
• formulate new questions
• draw these in an action plan
• compare data, models and solution routes
• making choices and giving arguments
• substantiate partial solutions
• make the planning explicit
• summarise again
• conclude what each of us will take up at the next meeting

Progress or growth-oriented coaching in consultation

Learning is not always a pleasure. Sometimes it is hard work, perhaps most of the time. However, it is working on something that is challenging, which you are interested in, which you choose to learn more about or which you can do better. Good coaching is also 'demanding coaching in consultation'. This is achieved through the continual questioning of content on the one hand and through the frequent cyclical nature of feedback dialogues on the other. In these feedback dialogues, the feedforward step takes an important place; it supports the learner to learn from feedback and thus grow.

Growth-oriented coaching starts with re-establishing the connection. Connection consists of mutual understanding, respect and attunement. It is the strengthening of the bond of trust that is necessary for learning. After all, learning is not possible in a situation of fear and distrust. Maintaining the connection is therefore a priority during the entire feedback dialogue.

Growth-oriented coaching means encouraging the learner to explicitly and purposefully take all steps in the feedback process in a dialogical manner (see the steps of a dialogical feedback process in Figure 8.1). Specifically, in order to stimulate deep learning, the feedback that has been cognitively and affectively processed by the learner is part of an action plan that the learner creates. This action plan stimulates and facilitates that the feedback is concretely put to work. The follow-up activities, in turn, are the input for new learning objectives set by the learner and thus the first step of a new feedback dialogue. Therefore, the action plan is an important tool in the feedforward step and as input for the new feed-up phase. As a coach, we stimulate the learner to use the action plan in this way, we stimulate planning, working step by step, dealing consciously with timing and the example questions for progress- or growth-oriented coaching questions are mentioned in Table 14.3.

Making the feedforward step explicit under the guidance of the coach not only increases the acceptance of using feedback dialogues, but also the usefulness becomes clear, the content is understood, and all this leads to positive emotions (affective reactions) during the learning process. This in turn leads to more depth, stronger integration and a feeling of flow. You want more, now that things are going so well you want to continue, you feel that you are on the track of a solution, your teammates explain new facts, concepts, relationships, structures, methods and so on.

Summarised: PCP coaching (progress and growth-oriented; content focused; process focused) is coaching aimed at growth/advancement, at depth/breakthrough and look through. On the other dimension are the

Table 14.3 Example questions for progress- or growth-oriented coaching

- What are your next steps
- When do you think you will have completed the next step?
- When can we review action 2 and 3 together?
- How much time do you need for the next part?
- Do you need anything else to be finished by Tuesday?
- What will you have ready next week?
- What will we discuss next week?
- How does your planning look?
- Are we on schedule?
- Who makes the adjustments to the planning?
- How will this contribute to your planned learning outcome?
- How do you see those actions being realised?
- Is it clear how we will proceed?

recurring phases in the feedback dialogue: connection, feed-up, feedback, feed-forward (see Figure 14.1).

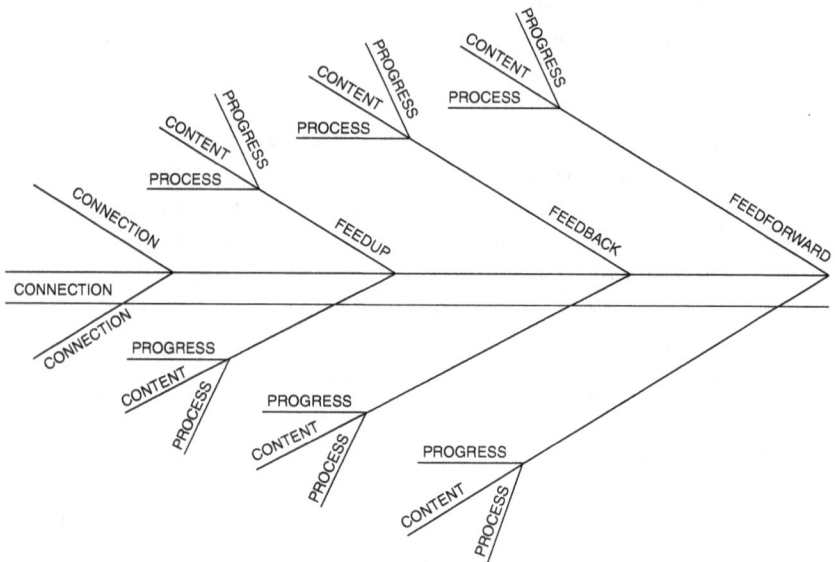

Figure 14.1 Schematic representation of PCP coaching.

Learning-oriented versus behaviour-oriented coaching

Learning-oriented PCP coaching is different from behaviour-oriented coaching, which a therapist practices, for example. In Table 14.4, we show the characteristics and the differences.

Table 14.4 Learning-oriented and behaviour-oriented coaching

Coaching	Behaviour-oriented coaching	Learning-oriented/PCP-coaching
	Short-term form of assistance, counselling	Long-term and development-oriented guidance and support
	Focused on specific behaviour or skills	Focused on learning competences (K, A, V) in authentic situations
	Meeting by appointment; re-enacting and reflecting on practical situations	Feedback dialogue at learner's request
	Intake to clarify expectations	Continuous feedback dialogues (weekly; 2 weekly) with connection, feed-up (where am I going?), feedback (how did it go?) and feedforward (what are the next steps?)
	Supporting	Focused on agency
	Personal performance	Progress-oriented coaching;
		Content-oriented coaching
		(in-depth and concept-oriented questions; solution-oriented questions; application in new situations; analysis; summarising/ synthesising; explaining/clarifying; schematic);
		Process-oriented coaching;
		Individual process and Team process
	With coach and client	With learning coach, peers and possibly practice coach/company representative
	Personal report by coach/ therapist	FeedPulse – reporting of the feedback dialogues by the learner

Conditions for successful coaching

Of course, there are also certain conditions to ensure successful coaching. According to Dochy, Gijbels, Segers and Van den Bossche (2022), the following conditions need to be taken into account:

1. A qualified coach or certified HILL coach.
2. PCP coaching is supported and encouraged by management; training opportunities are provided.
3. PCP coaching is integrated into the learner's learning process.

4. After a period of coaching, it will be checked whether both the personal goals set by the learner and the learning results set by the organisation have been achieved.
5. Sufficient time for coaching, preferably on a weekly basis. This also increases the learner's motivation to participate in the coaching process (Knight, 2009).

Practical examples and tools ▌▌▌

Assessment-as-Learning is booming, and many courses in recent years have attempted to give feedback the place it deserves. In this process, feedback is becoming the core of learning and also the core of assessment. In short, it is the energy supply for a powerful learning process that generates long-term impact.

The principles and findings from research in Chapters 1 and 2 of this book are brought to life here. We visited a number of programmes that have been implementing HILL for several years and have extensive experience with Assessment-as-Learning. We asked about the essence of their feedback approach.

DOI: 10.4324/9781003294139-18

The MoL

15

MSc learning and development in organisations

In 2009 the master's programme Management of Learning at Maastricht University, School of Business and Economics, started based on the HILL building blocks. Since 2019, this programme is called MSc Learning and Development in Organisations. The student population is very diverse, both in educational background and nationality. Each year, about 60 students participate in this master's programme. We asked initiator and founder Prof. Mien Segers how this programme works.

Can you give an example of how this programme fits in with the HILL model?

Mien: *A striking example is the project period. During eight weeks, the students act in teams of five to six as consultants for companies. Each team has one company as its client. The company presents its problem or challenge to the team and seeks a solution. An example of a problem that a company presents to a team is: a company doubts, on the basis of incidental information, whether the current traditional Performance Evaluation model matches the company's new 'employer brand'. During the project period, the teams are supervised by a coach from the School of Business and Economics and by a representative of the company, whom we call 'the client'. The coach stimulates and supports the process through continuous feedback dialogue throughout the project period. The client is responsible for access to company information (documents, employees, etc.) and enters into a continuous dialogue with its team about the approach and intermediate results.*

DOI: 10.4324/9781003294139-19

How does the feedback dialogue between a team and the coach start?

Mien: *Every week, two timeslots are established in which a team can schedule an appointment with the coach. It is the team's responsibility to book the appointment and to draw up an agenda for the meeting. The agenda of the meeting contains questions that the team would like to discuss. Seeking feedback is thus the start of the feedback dialogue. The questions are of various kinds. Some questions are about the team process. For example, the team doubts whether the division of tasks is efficient. Or one of the team members has the feeling that the team members have different ambitions with regard to the intended quality of the end product. Other questions are of a substantive nature. For example: the problem presented by the company is very vague and the more often it is discussed with the customer, the more unclear it becomes. How do we arrive at a question that can be answered or, in other words, how do we arrive at a clearly defined problem and, from there, a defined consultancy question? Another example: after defining the problem and the question, the team sees different perspectives that are relevant for tackling the question. For example, do you approach it from the perspective of leadership or from the perspective of an innovation? Which perspective do you choose and on the basis of which arguments? How do you balance the perspectives? Some questions are about the cooperation with the company. Example questions are: the customer reacts very slowly to mails. What do we do now? He actually already has the solution to the problem he presents to the team in his head and doesn't seem to be open to alternatives. How to deal with this?*

How does such a feedback dialogue work?

The team presents its questions and the coach starts a discussion with the team. The coach starts with question clarification, and through brainstorming together, the different answer options are listed and choices are made. Sometimes, during the brainstorming together, questions arise that cannot be answered immediately and that need further research. The team then draws up an action plan in dialogue with the coach.

In addition, the coach takes on the role of 'critical friend' and at the same time serves as a role model for critical reflection. For example, when ideas are put forward or decisions are taken, the coach asks questions such as why do you think this? What are your arguments? What are they based on? Are there alternatives?

What does such a feedback dialogue consist of?

Mien: *In a feedback dialogue, the following questions come up:*
  In the preliminary discussion of the feedback dialogue, in the team itself:

- *What is going well?*
- *Where do we get stuck?*
- *Where do we think we need support?*
- *What do we want to test with the coach/expert?*
- *Is our planning OK?*

  Actually, there are five phases in the actual feedback dialogue:

- *How are you doing? (Connection)*
- *Questions from the team.*
- *Where are you going? (Feed-up)*
- *How did it go? (Feedback)*
- *How do we approach the next steps? (Feedforward)*

  In the post discussion of the feedback dialogue in the team:

- *What do we take away from the conversation?*
- *What do we need to adjust?*
- *What do we need to find out?*
- *What will be included in the action plan?*
- *How will we approach it?*

Does the feedback dialogue only take place between the team and coach?

No. The weekly feedback meetings do take place between team and coach, planned and prepared by the team. In addition, there are two moments during the project period when teams enter into dialogue with each other. The first moment takes place when each team has written a draft of the project scoping note. In this project scoping note, the specific questions to which the customer expects an answer and the context of these questions, the expected deliverables, a risk analysis, a time schedule and a budget are recorded and approved by the customer. Prior to the feedback dialogue or this note, each team formulates the questions or points on which it would like to receive feedback from another team. During the team feedback dialogue, both teams discuss the feedback questions that have been raised. In addition to the feedback questions, a team can also take the space to put additional points on the agenda, for example, *certain parts of the scoping note they find particularly well worked out or for which they have a suggestion.*

A second moment is at the end of the project period when the outputs are ready in draft form. A fixed part of these deliverables is a project report for the company. In addition, the scoping note may state that the team generates other deliverables, such as a presentation for the company's management team, a flyer for customers and so on. As with the feedback dialogue on the project scoping note, each team submits its feedback questions to the other team with whom it is engaging in dialogue and these are the starting point of the conversation.

Do the teams also have feedback conversations with the customer?

At the start of the project period, the teams plan with the client how often and by what means they will consult with each other. Some consultation moments are informative, others have the character of a feedback dialogue. The teams are encouraged by the coach to engage in regular feedback dialogue with the client. On the one hand, the teams are encouraged to take the client along in the different steps of the analysis of the problem and the formulation of solution paths. The main objective is to check whether the client and the team understand each other, and thus to prevent the client (and thus the team) from being confronted with surprises at the end of the project period, with analyses, decisions and results that do not match the expectations. So, a case of expectation management in other words. On the other hand, the teams are encouraged to ask the customer for feedback on the process, on how the team is managing the project, how the communication between team and company is going.

Upon delivery of the deliverables, the team has a feedback meeting with the customer. Both the team and the client put items on the agenda for feedback. Content-related questions and process-related questions are discussed. This meeting takes about an hour.

Is there also a final feedback moment between the coach and team?

Yes, there is. After the delivery of the outputs and the feedback meeting with the client, the client and a coach who did not supervise the team in question review both the outputs and the feedback meeting. This involves using rubrics that were *discussed with the teams at the start of the project period. They are also regularly used during feedback meetings with the coach to guide the dialogue. Assessment thus takes place on the basis of a 360° feedback session that includes both the final product and the final presentation.*

The students receive the rubrics which indicate on various indicators at what level the team has performed by both the client and the coach. The examples are given and possible tips are formulated. During the so-called debriefing session, the team and its coach discuss, partly on the basis of the completed rubrics, what the team has learned in this project period, where they have grown. The central question in this meeting is: what will we take away from this project period, as a team and as individuals? This is an extremely valuable moment. On the one hand, it is about learning to deal with the feedback one has received via the rubrics and that is always an instructive moment, accepting that, even though you have worked really hard, the customer still has a few questions or concerns. On the other hand, this meeting helps to turn the experience into a real learning moment, a step in your professional development process as a student.

The MET learning hubs 16

The MET is a group of high-impact learning secondary schools, or better High Impact Learning that Lasts (HILL) learning hubs, in Belgium (St. Katelijne Wavre, Leuven and Tielt-Winge) that were realised by pioneers Elke Geuens and Griet Mertens (and later also Tinne De Beusscher, Martijn Roelen and others), in which Assessment-as-Learning gets hands and feet through a progress monitor and feedback conversations. The learning hubs used high-impact learning as a scientific basis and the practice of the Agora School as inspiration.

Pupils work continuously on challenges of their own choice and present their progress and results to peers and external parties.

We asked Griet Mertens and Tinne De Beusscher how they use feedback as a learning tool:

Griet: *We mainly give feedback verbally, but of course you cannot see that in the challenge monitor. What is written under 'feedback' in the challenge monitor is a summary of the verbal feedback that the other students and the coach give during the discussion. Most students write it down themselves in their challenge monitor (then it is under feedback), some students find writing down not so easy in the beginning and then the coach takes over (then it is in the margin under feedback from the coach). Actually, we don't give much written feedback. There is a record of the oral feedback that the student wants to take along, so that we can follow up together. This way, we know that students really understand their feedback and we are also sure that there is a concrete action plan that we follow up on together. In this way, feedback has a strong influence on what children do and how they do it. In this way, it becomes a powerful learning tool with long-term effects.*

DOI: 10.4324/9781003294139-20

How does such a feedback dialogue or coaching session work?

Every week, a pupil has about one or two coach conversations of 20–40 minutes. There, their progress and development is discussed. Usually they come with their own questions. The conversation then starts with getting on the same page, for example, How do you feel (about the task, today, etc.)? How does that come about?. After that, we always try to start on a positive note with questions such as: What is going well? What are you proud of? Followed by self-feedback: How did it go? What did you like and what did you dislike? What have you already achieved (product)? How did you go about it (process)? Where are you still stuck?/How did you get there?/What do you need to continue? What have others (coaches, pupils, parents, outsiders) meant in your process? And then encourage students to seek feedback themselves: Have you asked/told anyone this before?

We actually try to challenge and frame continuously, and we also give feedback as a learning coach where the emphasis is on positive feedback: discuss product/process and give tops (medals) and tips (mission): What I have recorded/seen as a coach is …/I understand that you …

Then we make clear agreements about how we will proceed: When will we return to this? And we usually conclude by returning to the essence of the coaching conversation: What do you take away from this? Can you summarise? What does your work plan look like?

If it is a coaching conversation in response to a presentation, we also add to that: How do you think you can raise your presentation to a higher level (in terms of content, presentation style, interaction with the audience, depth, broad scope, etc.)? Do you feel you have reached everyone?

What is the effect of the feedback dialogues/coaching conversations?

Tinne: *These very regular and continuous coaching conversations create a strong bond, interaction between the coach and the pupil, through which pupils can build a strong trust in themselves and in others. This is necessary to be able to learn and dare to learn.*

Believing in yourself and experiencing that others also believe in you (including the learning coach) enables inner growth as a person, growth in learning and depth of content, growth in curiosity to discover and growth in courage. In this way, you are also on the ball. As a learning coach, you also sense immediately when a pupil is not feeling well (personally, in terms of seeking and processing information, with and or by others, etc.). You can respond to this immediately, try to help, involve others in the process, so that together you can ensure that the pupil has every opportunity to continue to develop and learn.

Our children also learn to a large extent to 'self-evaluate', to reflect on their own learning process, to think problem-solving. Together with the learning coach, this is constantly being practised, so that they get to know themselves better and can respond to it themselves, adapt to it and face challenges on their own level. Positive feedback makes you grow, makes you blossom, which in turn makes you more open to learning more, further. However, equally important are the missions (read: critical feedback). Given in confidence, knowing what you can still work on, how you can get further make you able to bring yourself, your work to a higher level. You get to know yourself and know what you are good at and what you are less good at. You grow towards making a conscious choice for your future. You will be seen and heard! In your work and in your being! Coach conversations are a form of respect in both directions.

Gilde Training Programmes about well-being

17

Gilde Training Programmes is a career centre in Limburg. In the Venray location, department of Welfare, Jolanda Rijnders and Janske Castelijns are the driving forces behind the High Impact Learning that Lasts (HILL) implementation since 2016. Soon after, Hay Freriks and Alex van Vliet also came up with brilliant initiatives such as the HILL ambassadorship for students and the coaching innovation for teachers (by students, by the way).

How did you create the feedback dialogue with impact?

Jolanda and Janske: *Because of our penchant for high-impact education, in 2016 we as a welfare team took up the following challenge: 'We stop teaching, tests and grades; from now on we are going to give feedback'. Feedback dialogues and also peer feedback have since gained a fundamental place in our welfare training programs. On the one hand, at more formal and planned moments, such as during peer assessments, learning team discussions and during study progress interviews. On the other hand, an informal feedback culture has emerged; a learning culture in which students and learning coaches naturally question and give feedback to each other. We have abandoned the idea that students first need to be trained in order to do this well. We noticed that students quickly learn how to give and seek feedback by 'just doing it'. They learn this during teamwork and notice how meaningful and also pleasant it is to work together as equal learning partners; a natural process in which you as learning coaches are role models and invite each other to give feedback. The change as a team was not always easy, because it takes a while for new students to get the 'right taste'*

DOI: 10.4324/9781003294139-21

and then it is tempting to fall back into the traditional role of teacher. However, by making feedback a learning theme at team level as well, we managed to maintain the course well. We organise intervision based on our own urgencies, ask students to mirror us and, as coaches, we offer each other support. Difficult issues are no longer avoided either but discussed and taken up in a professional dialogue.

Voerman's work on learning-enhancing feedback has inspired us to pay attention in feedback dialogues not only to the content and the process but also to the learning mode and the personal qualities of students. Being able to openly discuss the emotions that arise during learning, the personal qualities and the growth that the student experiences, in our experience, strongly promotes the involvement and belief in the student's own abilities. To stimulate personal growth even more, we have recently started to coach explicitly on 'personal mastery', which is operationalised in core competencies such as brainpower, guts and flexibility. As a result, we see an increased urge to seek more depth in content and to try out new process steps. You see students stepping out of their comfort zone more and more easily and then consciously stepping into the learning zone. The involvement in each one's learning process is also increasing visibly. For example, students like to join in with each other's work placement discussions or the learning coaches' performance reviews in order to spar and give feedback.

So what are the characteristics of a powerful feedback dialogue?

Janske and Jolanda: *A powerful feedback dialogue has the following key features for us:*

- *A planned or spontaneous meeting (just-in-time) between a learning coach (or peer coach) and a learner (or learning team).*
- *The starting point is 'connection': there is mutual openness and equality.*
- *There is an urgency: the learner has an urge to further explore his 'task'.*
- *Both the learning product and the learning process are explored, with attention also for the personal development.*
- *Through self-feedback and learning coach-feedback, the learner himself comes to insights and new starting points.*
- *Feedback from the learning coach consists mainly of questions.*
- *The dialogues are cyclical, with a look back and a look forward to new, self-chosen actions (agency).*
- *The dialogue sets in motion an ongoing process of reflection and motivates the learner to go deeper and take action.*

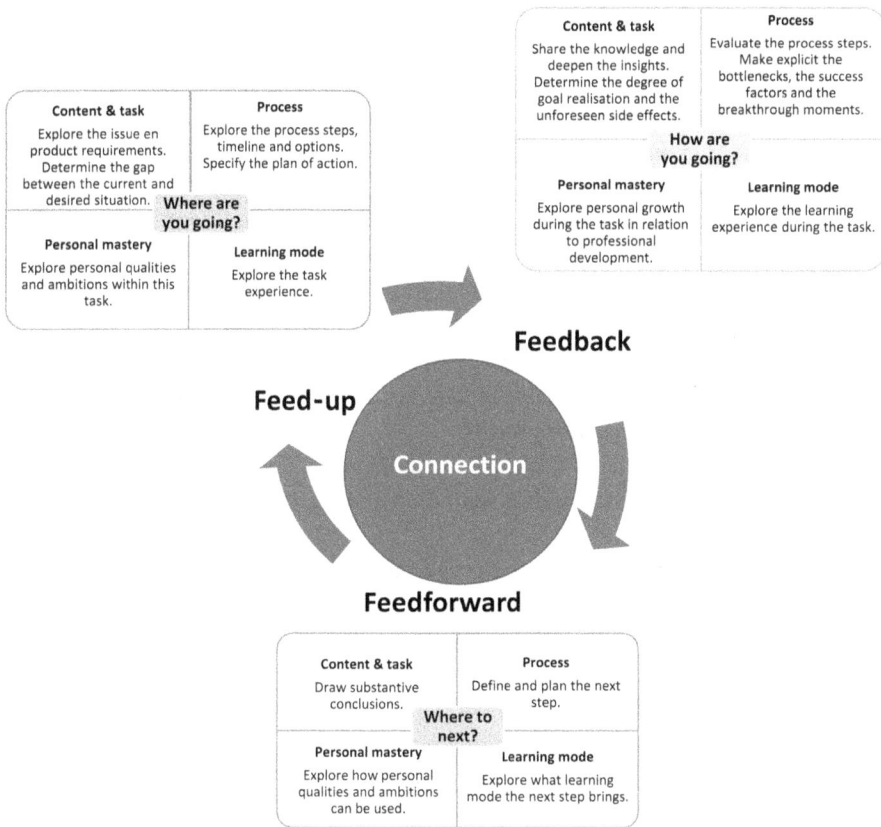

Figure 17.1 Characteristics of a powerful feedback dialogue.

- *The learner feels capable of taking further action (self-efficacy).*
- *This is a two-way street: both the learning coach and the learner share their questions and (new) insights and inspire each other.*

Summarised in Figure 17.1.

What is a learning coach required to do?

Jolanda and Janske: *A tour through the welfare team (approx. 25 people) shows that most of them feel more like learning coaches than teachers, explaining that they are no longer in front of the class to say 'how it is and how it should be' but move among the students and explore together.*

The ideal learning coach in our opinion:

- *Starts with sincere attention, appreciation and trust (basic attitude).*
- *Levels with the learner and goes deeper in order to reach the next level.*
- *Is committed to the learner and pays attention to their well-being, emotions and learning mode.*
- *Sees, names and values the uniqueness of the learner and relates it to his/her professional identity.*
- *Challenges the learner to step out of their comfort zone and confronts them.*
- *Sets high and challenging expectations for both the content and the process.*
- *Asks questions and taps into other perspectives.*
- *Allows the learner to give feedback first and then any learning partners.*
- *Supervises the peer feedback process.*
- *Uses meta-feedback: feedback on giving feedback.*
- *Gives measured feedback, in line with the question, without overruling the feedback of others.*
- *Lets the learner give meaning to the collected feedback.*
- *Invites the learner to summarise their reflections and record them in their own words.*
- *Checks whether he understands the learner correctly and invites the learner to make his own checks.*
- *Also learns from and with the learner himself.*
- *Explains 'the why' of his approach.*
- *Is never ALL-knowing, but rather NOT-knowing, PART-knowing or ALSO-knowing and is therefore a substantive sparring partner and role model.*
- *Ensures THAT learning takes place, but not WHAT learning takes place.*
- *Can put things into perspective and uses humour.*
- *Reflects on his/her own coaching and knows his/her own possibilities and limits.*

What are the effects of this feedback approach?

We notice that our students value a good relationship with the learning coach and with their peers. We also see that our feedback approach contributes to strengthening the mutual relationships. The effects of our approach for the learner can be summarised in the following points. The learner:

- *Seeks more depth in content by consulting richer and more diverse sources.*
- *Becomes more aware of his own direction and possibilities.*
- *Will try out new possibilities.*

- *Has more insight into where he/she stands and how he/she can move forward.*
- *Steps faster out of the comfort zone and into the learning zone.*
- *Taps into his/her own network more quickly.*
- *Will automatically give feedback and coach others.*
- *Challenges the learning coach to think more deeply and explore new paths.*
- *Becomes more critical.*
- *Will ask for depth in feedback.*
- *Shows more mutual involvement.*
- *Feels appreciated for who he/she is in his/her entirety.*
- *Cooperates more constructively.*
- *Gets 'hungry for feedback'.*
- *Quickly assumes a professional role.*
- *Is less dependent on the 'judgement' and expertise of the teacher/coach.*
- *Is better able to value his/her own work.*

Avans HR academy   18

The Human Resource Management (HRM) programme of Avans University of Applied Sciences is part of the Academy for General and Financial Management (AAFM) in Breda. In the past years, there have been strong Hill impulses by Hill certified trainer Charlotte Vermond, but also innovator Herman van Blitterswijk, and passionate coaches like Erik Woering, Vincent Verwaal, Richard Vos and others.

Erik Woering is currently the Human Resource Management coach there.

Erik: *Our education focuses on learning in a realistic task environment. This is based on the idea that education in which learning by doing tasks that resemble professional tasks plays a major role is effective for the development of the ability to act (acting and reflecting).*

We apply these seven HILL building blocks in our teaching from the junior semester onwards. By working with current professional issues and a high degree of involvement of the principals, we create a high degree of urgency and learner agency (self-management). Students work together both individually and in teams and learn in different settings where knowledge sharing and peer feedback are important components (action and knowledge sharing and collaboration and coaching). Assessment at the end of a semester shifts to continuous feedback (Assessment-as-Learning) during the semester, by frequently conducting so-called FeedPulse conversations in which the learning development is monitored. The lecturers strive for higher professionalism through stronger teamwork in a learning organisation and a highly dynamic educational approach. The lecturers constantly redesign their teaching (partly as a result of evaluations with students), continuously learn from colleagues and ceaselessly share their knowledge and skills.

DOI: 10.4324/9781003294139-22

Are real tasks the core of the learning process?

Erik: *The development and implementation of our education is closely intertwined with working on professionally authentic assignments for clients in the field. As a study programme, we apply the following principles, partly based on the building blocks of the HILL model:*

- *Education is focused on professional (HRM) and personal development.*
- *Education consists mainly of professional assignments. The study programme enters into close cooperation with the professional field in order to obtain professionally authentic assignments.*
- *The education is agile, allowing us to respond quickly and flexibly to the needs of the students and the field.*
- *The education is varied. To continually stimulate and motivate students, the education is varied and uses different forms of teaching in which ICT can be a tool.*
- *Education is flexible. The professional field can have issues carried out at short notice, with varying lead times. In addition, the structure of the education system allows students to work together in multidisciplinary teams with HRM students from other years and students from other study programmes.*
- *There is a variety of working methods that fit in with the professional assignment and the needs of the student.*
- *English is integrated in the first two years of the HRM curriculum. The teacher-coach decides, in consultation with students, fellow teacher-coaches and external clients, which part(s) of an assignment will be delivered in English. The language coach advises and inspires both students and teacher-coaches regarding the possibilities of practising English during a course of study in a particular semester. Based on that advice and/or the students' needs, the language coach offers workshops and training sessions aimed at developing writing and speaking skills.*

So what do the authentic assignments look like?

- *We work with current issues and assignments from the field, which means we are faced with themes that are relevant to the field at that time. This way, the education is always up-to-date. It is well known that working with authentic vocational tasks enhances the learning process.*
- *Assignments guide theory and skills, in the sense that relevant information is sought in the assignment (what is already known about this?) and relevant skills are addressed. Students search themselves for literature that is needed. Because the themes are topical, the theory that is used is also valuable for the*

future HR professional. The coach helps to determine what suitable literature to use and adjusts where necessary in order to use the latest insights and to consult good quality sources.

- *The assignments are true to the profession, recognisable and promote independence. Assignments have quality as far as content is concerned if they call for action by students in order to learn. Assignments promote learning dynamics.*
- *Assignments are meaningful and deep learning takes place when students want to learn.*
- *Personal development, research skills and sustainable development are an integral part of our way of working.*

What then is the relationship between the coach and the student?

The student feels seen by both teachers and fellow students. This is created by a culture in which teachers and students have an equal relationship with each other. The teacher and student show genuine interest in each other and dare to address each other where necessary.

On the one hand, students are self-directed and take their own responsibility. The programme encourages the student during the programme to become more self-directed and to take more responsibility. The student has an active role in this and is the owner of his own learning process: student in the lead. The teacher has a coaching role. This role is fulfilled in any case during individual talks and joint meetings. The coach listens, asks questions and, where necessary, encourages students to learn together in the learning community.

On the other hand, the teacher is a coach and an expert. The student takes responsibility, asks questions, is critical and is open to feedback. The instructor has various roles. In the first instance, he or she is a learning coach. He or she asks questions that make the student think for himself or herself and come to an answer. In addition, the teacher can at times fulfil the role of expert.

What about Assessment-as-Learning and continuous feedback and feedforward?

An important building block from Dochy's HILL model that we use in assessment is 'Assessment-as-Learning'. With some regularity, teacher-coaches have so-called FeedPulse conversations with the student to follow the progress of his learning process. Learning and evaluation (assessment) are intertwined: each evaluation moment (feedback from the teacher-coach) is at the same time a learning opportunity that results in new knowledge and insights to take along for the continuation of an assignment (feedforward).

In addition to the individual feedback meetings, the teacher-coach organises so-called group checkpoints, in which feedback and feedforward take place at group level. Students also organise mutual feedback sessions and use self-assessment and peer feedback.

In each semester, students are confronted with different assignments, clients, teacher coaches and fellow students and thus receive rich and varied feedback on their learning process. They include this feedback and their own reflection on it in their portfolio.

Students choose assignments that they find interesting and from which they can learn a lot and collect evidence with which they can demonstrate that they have met the relevant QC. The evidence and individual reflections (oral, written, audio and video recordings etc.) are included in a personal portfolio. The expected result will be determined together with the clients. For each assignment, a translation is made into professional products to be delivered, into which knowledge and skills should be developed and the way in which individual testing will take place, on the basis of the core competence standardisation. For this, a typology is used and the input from the above described norming sessions.

Fontys ICT open

Frank Haverkort is curriculum owner of the Information and Communication Technology (ICT) and Infrastructure programme in Eindhoven. The programme has had a HILL variant for many years. Pioneers of the open programme included HILL-certified trainers Eric Slaets and Britt Dingens as well as Martijn Ruissen and director Ad Vissers.

Frank: *At Fontys ICT open, students work with learning outcomes. They get feedback (feed-up and feedforward) on the learning process and on the product they deliver. Sometimes, they deliver multiple products for a learning outcome. The products handed in are often growth documents (becoming more and more complete). Feedback is provided or asked for through the learning and management system we use (Canvas by Instructure) and discuss it with the students. We also provide frequent verbal feedback during the periods and students use the FeedPulse programme in which they express the feedback they have received themselves.*

How do you use feedback then?

Frank: *We use feedback to make remarks/indications about the submitted work, feed-up to see where the student is now and feedforward to give and discuss the next step(s) in the development. In the written feed-up, we introduced a developmental scale to show where the student is in his development.*

For which assignments is feedback used?

Frank: *We give feedback on individual assignments as well as group assignments. Questions that are answered during the feedback dialogues with students are:*

- *What is going well? What are you satisfied with and why?*
- *What needs more attention or what could be better?*
- *What is the next step (what do you still need to do) in order to be able to demonstrate the learning outcome?*
- *In conclusion: do you know how to proceed and what will be agreed?*

In teacher training sessions, we provide the following table to give attention to all forms of feedback. As an example a completed table.

	Feed-up	Feedback	Feedforward
	What is the student's goal? "Where am I going?"	*How is the student doing so far (progression towards the goal set)?*	*What steps must the student take to reach the goal?*
Task			
How well the task is understood and/or performed	The intention is that you write a readable report	The explanation of your choices is missing, describe them here	Write short and concise sentences in your document to make it easier to read
	At the end of the semester, make sure you can create an OO design using UML diagrams	I think you still do not fully understand how a microcontroller works	For the design, you should also include a use case diagram, class diagram, sequence diagram and a state diagram

(Continued)

Process

The main process needed to understand and/or perform the task	Make sure that within the professional task everyone contributes proportionally to the documentation	I see that you have started slowly, because you have not handed in everything yet	Next time, make sure you and your group mates agree on who does what and when
	You are able to build a professional relationship with your stakeholders	I see that you have been working well, even completing the in-depth assignments to a good level	I recommend that you involve the stakeholders in your issue in good time

Self-regulation

Self-direction and ownership of the learning process	What are the objectives for this semester?	What have you achieved so far from your professional task objectives?	What would you like to do to improve?
	What do you want to achieve for yourself with the pro task?	To what extent have you realised your personal goals within the professional task?	Talk to your semester coach, subject teacher and fellow students about ways to keep challenging yourself

Person

Personal evaluations and feelings about the student. Do not use or use in moderation!	Make sure you use your creativity	How creative you are!	You will definitely learn!

Fontys ICT open   19

Frank Haverkort is the curriculum owner of the ICT and Infrastructure programme in Eindhoven. The programme has had a High Impact Learning
that Lasts (HILL) variant for many years. Pioneers of the open programme
included HILL-certified trainers Eric Slaets and Britt Dingens as well as
Martijn Ruissen and director Ad Vissers.

Frank: *At Fontys ICT open, students work with learning outcomes. They get
feedback (feed-up and feedforward) on the learning process and on the product
they deliver. Sometimes, they deliver multiple products for a learning outcome. The
products handed in are often growth documents (becoming more and more complete). Feedback is provided or asked for through the learning and management
system we use (Canvas by Instructure) and discuss it with the students. We also
provide frequent verbal feedback during the periods and students use the FeedPulse
programme in which they express the feedback they have received themselves.*

How do you use feedback then?

Frank: *We use feedback to make remarks/indications about the submitted work,
feed-up to see where the student is now and feedforward to give and discuss the next
step(s) in the development. In the written feed-up, we introduced a developmental
scale to show where the student is in his development.*

For which assignments is feedback used?

Frank: *We give feedback on individual assignments as well as group assignments.*

DOI: 10.4324/9781003294139-23

Questions that are answered during the feedback dialogues with students are:

- *What is going well? What are you satisfied with and why?*
- *What needs more attention or what could be better?*
- *What is the next step (what do you still need to do) in order to be able to demonstrate the learning outcome?*
- *In conclusion: Do you know how to proceed and what will be agreed?*

In teacher training sessions, we provide the following table to give attention to all forms of feedback, as an example a completed table.

	Feed-up	Feedback	Feedforward
	What is the student's goal? 'Where am I going?'	*How is the student doing so far (progression towards the goal set)?*	*What steps must the student take to reach the goal?*
Task			
How well the task is understood and/or performed	The intention is that you write a readable report	The explanation of your choices is missing, describe them here	Write short and concise sentences in your document to make it easier to read
	At the end of the semester, make sure you can create an OO design using UML diagrams	I think you still do not fully understand how a microcontroller works	For the design, you should also include a use case diagram, class diagram, sequence diagram and a state diagram
Process			
The main process needed to understand and/or perform the task	Make sure that within the professional task everyone contributes proportionally to the documentation	I see that you have started slowly, because you have not handed in everything yet	Next time, make sure you and your group mates agree on who does what and when
	You are able to build a professional relationship with your stakeholders	I see that you have been working well, even completing the in-depth assignments to a good level	I recommend that you involve the stakeholders in your issue in good time

(Continued)

Self-regulation

Self-direction and ownership of the learning process	What are the objectives for this semester?	What have you achieved so far from your professional task objectives?	What would you like to do to improve?
	What do you want to achieve for yourself with the pro task?	To what extent have you realised your personal goals within the professional task?	Talk to your semester coach, subject teacher and fellow students about ways to keep challenging yourself

Person

Personal evaluations and feelings about the student. Do not use or use in moderation!	Make sure you use your creativity	How creative you are!	You will definitely learn!

Some further tips and answering some frequently asked questions

IV

Feedback dialogues   **20**
Where do I get the time?

Time is a tricky customer when we think from the structure of traditional training. Rethinking the commitment of employees is necessary if we want to set up a training programme in which the power of feedback can be optimally realised. Time is most being spent on two tasks that teachers/ trainers perform: teaching and testing. Sometimes you hear that teachers spend on average more than 20 hours a week on these two tasks. Of course, this includes preparation, as well as making test questions, making tests, calibrating, taking tests, correcting and so on.
Where do we find the necessary time?

1. Give teachers back their expert role.
   As research shows, the long-term effectiveness of teaching is very low. And, teaching has become too much like reading out PowerPoint slides. Learners have little use for them and do not pay much attention to them. In-depth explanations by an expert are only relevant if the learner asks for them and if the explanation is as spontaneous as possible and linked to a concrete case. Flash lectures (explanations by an expert at the request of, for example, at least 30 learners who are given an inter-active session one day after the request) are thus the best way to make learners understand difficult content. High impact learning courses use flash lectures, but also knowledge sharing, expert questioning (external experts), deep-question meetings and so on. We offer space for learners to request and receive one to two flash lectures per week and/or we leave space for students to sign up for 'challenges' in which they tackle and unravel a complex challenge together with a learning coach. In this kind of 'knowledge sharing', students explain the knowledge they

DOI: 10.4324/9781003294139-25

acquire to each other and select and apply the relevant knowledge. All other lessons are dropped and become work time, study time and feedback time.

2. Go fully for Assessment-as-Learning.

All tests are disappearing and assessment is now preferably based on programme or curriculum level (so-called programmatic or curriculum targeted assessment; Baartman, van Schilt-Mol, & Van der Vleuten, 2020) and on monitoring of development, feedback, products, papers, portfolio and learning analytics. This is also possible within existing course units, but the smaller the size of these units, the more difficult it becomes to ensure the adequate development of the cycle of feedback dialogues and the assessment of final results in a motivating and natural way.

Of course, Assessment-as-Learning also takes time, but the integration of this assessment in the learning process, the link to direct content and applications and the fact that feedback is an essential part, bring significant benefits. Not only is there a much stronger knowledge assurance, it also leads to a considerable saving in time (no question banks; no massive correction time, etc.). The time freed up can be fully invested in feedback dialogues.

Courses that make the change from test-based learning to high impact learning and a system of Assessment-as-Learning all attest to the fact that the change is a zero-sum operation in terms of time and effort, at least on the instructor's side. The learner's side is of course not a zero operation: the learner invests more time in the feedback dialogues (preparation, reporting), in planning, in carrying out tasks/challenges, in preparing, for example, the assessment interviews or the portfolio, in study time, in preparing and giving presentations and so on. That is what we were looking for, right?

How do people experience feedback dialogues in practice?   **21**

Research by Voerman, Meijer, Korthagen and Simons (2012) into teachers' feedback practices shows that little positive feedback is generally given, that explanations are often lacking and that feedback is only given after learning activities have been completed. There is therefore a great deal of reason to train instructors.

Ten years ago, Voerman and Faber (2010) produced a model for didactic coaching. This already contained a number of good guidelines for coaching so that it promotes learning:

- Feedback is as specific as possible, but not too long.
- Feedback is more about what is right, rather than what is wrong. And this in a ratio of about three times as much positive feedback as negative feedback.
- Feedback has a past, a present and a future: feedback indicates what is already better than before and how it can be improved in the future.

The basic characteristics of didactic coaching were put into three terms by Voerman and Faber (2010): observe, question and check.

We start from what we see (a product, an intermediate product, behaviour, an approach, etc.) and then we ask questions (or name them or give feedback) in order to reflect on the information or questions given. Finally, we check whether it is received positively, whether there is a plan of action and whether there is progress. But in practice, more seems to be needed. Castelijns (2017) clearly indicates that it is essential to dare to let go and to work on the basis of trust (see also Hattie, 2012). Expertise in giving

DOI: 10.4324/9781003294139-26

specific dimensions of feedback with the right timing is also highly desirable (Hattie & Timperley, 2007).

What do lecturers and students themselves say about weekly feedback dialogues?

Castelijns found that, in her innovation project, both students and instructors like to have 'feedback conversations', that is dialogues. Castelijns (2017) writes:

> Learners also have positive experiences with feedback conversations. They regularly talk about the need for two-way traffic, because they like being given the opportunity to respond to feedback and to explain their perspective. According to both students and lecturers, a coaching approach by lecturers is ideal; they mention feedback in the form of asking questions, being guided to insights and at the same time being given sufficient tools to tackle learning tasks. (p. 19)

And further:

> A lecturer shares the good practice of leaving the choice of whether or not to receive feedback to the student. According to the students, offering a choice is a good option because it appeals to their own responsibilities. (p. 19)

With regard to the fundamental attitude of lecturers, students in Castelijns' research found that it is important to have a close, equal relationship with lecturers. They are then more open to feedback and value it more. After all, students often have an explicit need for trust.

Finally, Castelijns also talks about the need to be all seen and also to get feedback when things are going well. It is not only teams that are not yet well on their way that need feedback conversations but also teams that have not yet got their act together. 'Teachers recognise this picture', Castelijns writes, 'they express the need to look at the students much more with positive glasses on, from a fundamental attitude of being self-learners in dialogue with all students'.

Professionalisation of teachers with respect to feedback

22

Teachers are often familiar with giving feedback, but not with feedback dialogues. Consistent training and intervision to arrive at effective feedback dialogues seems to us a must in which teachers learn other habits: very frequent dialogues, from a vision of negotiation, from an equal position on the one hand and as a 'real' expert on the other, together in co-construction with teams and individuals, feedback from multiple parties, using feedback as part of Assessment-as-Learning, documenting feedback (by learners), following up feedback together on the basis of action plans and so on.

We have already written: there is much reason for teacher training in feedback dialogues. At Gilde Wellbeing Training Programmes Venray, they started with 'basic attitude' as an important theme for professionalisation and the teacher made the link to the core values that were formulated by the team at the start of the HILL pilot as a basis for working with students.

In the project by Castelijns and colleagues, lecturers indicated that sharing knowledge and experiences and involving students in this learning process are indispensable in order to learn to give learning-enhancing feedback. Teachers also wanted to train their coaching skills (e.g. through intervision) in order to learn how to give learning-enhancing feedback in an adequate way. To this end, external process supervision was hired.

In Castelijns' project, learning-enhancing feedback started from a positive fundamental attitude: instructors approach students on the basis of trust and appreciation. To this end, lecturers must take on a coaching role, whereby learning-enhancing feedback is expressed mainly in reflective questions and in checking how the feedback is received and how it is dealt with further. Figure 22.1 gives an overview of the insights gained concerning feedback during the orientation phase of the professionalisation process.

DOI: 10.4324/9781003294139-27

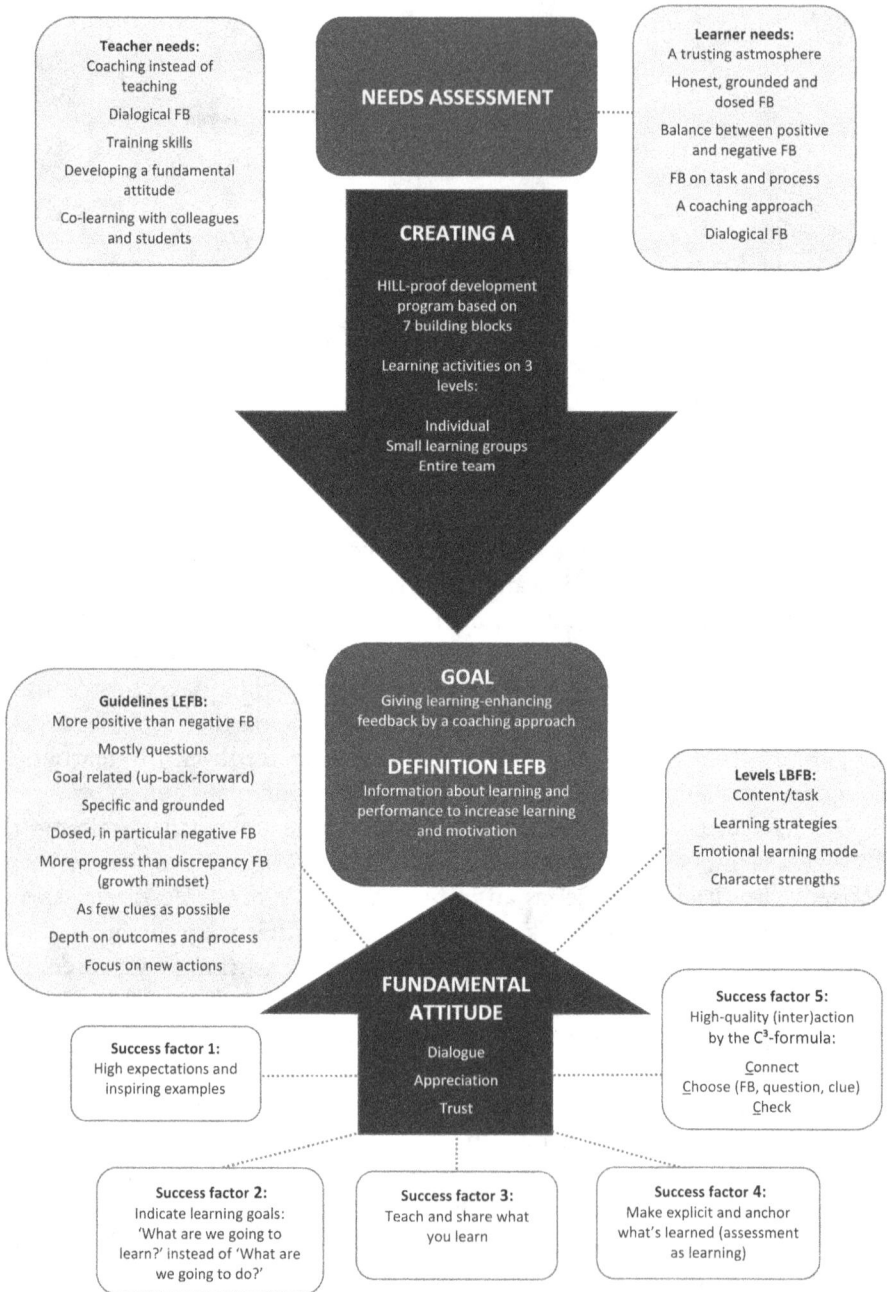

Teacher needs:
Coaching instead of teaching

Dialogical FB

Training skills

Developing a fundamental attitude

Co-learning with colleagues and students

NEEDS ASSESSMENT

Learner needs:
A trusting astmosphere

Honest, grounded and dosed FB

Balance between positive and negative FB

FB on task and process

A coaching approach

Dialogical FB

CREATING A

HILL-proof development program based on 7 building blocks

Learning activities on 3 levels:

Individual
Small learning groups
Entire team

GOAL
Giving learning-enhancing feedback by a coaching approach

DEFINITION LEFB
Information about learning and performance to increase learning and motivation

Guidelines LEFB:
More positive than negative FB

Mostly questions

Goal related (up-back-forward)

Specific and grounded

Dosed, in particular negative FB

More progress than discrepancy FB (growth mindset)

As few clues as possible

Depth on outcomes and process

Focus on new actions

Levels LBFB:
Content/task

Learning strategies

Emotional learning mode

Character strengths

FUNDAMENTAL ATTITUDE

Dialogue

Appreciation

Trust

Success factor 1:
High expectations and inspiring examples

Success factor 5:
High-quality (inter)action by the C³-formula:

Connect
Choose (FB, question, clue)
Check

Success factor 2:
Indicate learning goals: 'What are we going to learn?' instead of 'What are we going to do?'

Success factor 3:
Teach and share what you learn

Success factor 4:
Make explicit and anchor what's learned (assessment as learning)

Abbreviations: FB = feedback, LEFB = learning-enhancing feedback

Figure 22.1 Concept map insights from the orientation phase professionalisation (Castelijns, 2017).

The entire process they went through with their teaching team, team of learning coaches, is plotted in the table below (Castelijns, 2017). At various stages of the teacher professionalisation, there was an intensive injection by the HILL Academy (www.highimpactlearningthatlasts.com).

Design steps	Findings of the design team	Draft decisions
1. Instructional problems Can the performance problem be (partially) solved with the help of instructions?	– The needs assessment has shown that the teachers feel gaps in their own knowledge and skills to give learning-enhancing feedback; they themselves feel the urgency to enrich their feedback repertoire through a professionalisation programme	– A professionalisation path, that is training, is being designed
2. Learner characteristics What are the learner and context characteristics?	• The change management characterisation shows that individual learning preferences dominate discovery and participation. At the team level, new learning patterns are needed to achieve transformative learning • All the teachers are motivated to participate; at the same time, the prior knowledge and experienced learning competencies will differ among them • The course takes place within the context of the HILL innovation process • The school is the physical learning context, which means that facilities such as a beamer, laptop, various rooms, board, etc., are available. There are four team sessions of 4 hours • The transfer context is ideal; what has been learned can immediately be applied in practice	– Interventions full of (inter)action, reflection and awareness of one's own learning mode are the core elements for achieving transformative learning – There is a link to previous knowledge – To strengthen the link to the HILL, a 'HILL-proof' design is made, which means that the building blocks are recognisable in the design – All the accumulated knowledge about learning-enhancing feedback will be addressed during the course, with sufficient room to work on your own learning goals

(Continued)

3. Task analysis What knowledge, attitudes and skills need to be learned?	• Knowledge of the rules of thumb and success factors for learning-enhancing feedback and the four dimensions • A positive basic attitude and active learning • Skills to apply rules of thumb and success factors for learning-enhancing feedback and the four dimensions	– The concept map and didactic coaching are used to draw up a task analysis, divided into knowledge, attitude and skills
4. Instructional objectives What are the learning objectives?	– The main goal is that in May the teachers will give learning-enhancing feedback from a coaching role – Learning goals can be formulated with regard to knowledge, attitude and skills	• The main objective is divided into six learning objectives relating to knowledge, attitude and skills. With the help of the task analysis, these learning objectives are operationalised into concrete performance indicators • The learning objectives form the intended outcome or frame of reference
5. Content sequencing In what order are the instructions offered?	– An integral build-up from less to more complex knowledge, attitude and skills	– To keep the overall view, the draft folder is used as an epitome, that is, an overview from which to constantly zoomed in and out
6. Instructional strategies What is the best way to learn to achieve the learning goals?	• By preparing learners well for instruction (effective pre-instructional strategies) • By connectivist instructional strategies: meaningful, interactive learning in networks through theory, demonstration, practice, coaching, feedback and knowledge sharing • By alternating team sessions with interventions at the subgroup and individual level	• The basic attitude, dimensions, success factors and guidelines for learning-enhancing feedback and the HILL building blocks are continuously used by those responsible for instruction, either implicitly or explicitly • Team sessions are used for (interactive) learning. Theory is not transferred frontally, but studied individually and then actively applied during team sessions

(Continued)

	• By using the power of exemplary behaviour and applying the principle of 'practice what you preach' • The above coincides with applying the building blocks of HILL	• Fixed subgroups are formed during the programme, the so-called learning teams • Individuals draw up a personal development plan (PDP) and personal activity plan (PAP) based on a personal baseline measurement • Students are used as learning partners
7. Designing the message How can the learning content best be translated into a design plan?	– By distributing the learning content across the four team sessions, taking into account the integral structure of design step 5	– Design plan is determined in outline, with sufficient flexible space for input from the teachers along the way
8. Development of instructional materials What points of attention are important when designing the instructional materials?	• Use concise and stimulating language • Use a consistent and clear layout • Offer no more, but also no less materials than necessary to follow the course well	• PowerPoint is used during the team sessions to visualise the instructions • If necessary, extra instructions are handed out on paper • All instructional materials are also published in the ELE • Starting from didactic coaching
9. Evaluation instruments How is evaluation carried out?	– By interim evaluations: what are the experiences with the design? – Through a baseline measurement and a final measurement: to what extent are the learning objectives mastered before/ after the course?	• Team sessions 1–3 conclude with an interim evaluation • A questionnaire will be developed using the frame of reference to carry out a baseline and final measurement

Quality, supportive and constructive feedback also appears to be essential for professional development. The reflection of professionals is an important part of the feedback process and should be a two-way or multiway dialogue. Giving feedback should therefore be a continuous conversation between learner, professional, peers and trainers.

Based on the above process of professionalisation with regard to feedback, we once again come to the recommendations given in Box 22.1.

BOX 22.1

Recommendations for feedback

a. Reflection and feedback must form an integral part of a feedback dialogue.
b. Feedback dialogues are cyclical and compare current and previous products.
c. Feedback should take place as soon as possible after an activity in order to maximise the benefits.
d. Feedback should be frequent, supportive, facilitative and encourage self-reflection; it should be specific, relevant and non-judgmental.
e. Dialogue should provide confirmation that the learner understands the feedback.
f. Feedback should include an action plan (from the learner) for future development.
g. A solid professionalisation programme for teachers with regard to feedback dialogues is an essential basis for successful innovation.

Software to support feedback dialogues

23

The world is drowning in apps and software packages, even when it comes to organising feedback. However, just like scientific research, much of this software is still submerged in the classical transfer paradigm. A number of tools transcend that and sometimes take a very nice step towards educating the future. A selection of these tools can be found below.

FeedPulse

FeedPulse is a tool by Drieam that is used to put Assessment-as-Learning into practice (see Figure 23.1). Students are provided with development-oriented feedback at several moments. The various measuring moments are learning moments for the student (and teacher) and can provide valuable information about the development. Students themselves process the oral feedback in FeedPulse. This activates them and makes them partly responsible for their own development. Moreover, there is a clear check whether students understand the feedback correctly and are able to work with it. Because the feedback from multiple measurement moments can be recorded in the tool, an overview of the students' development over time is created. This makes it easy for the teacher to monitor the learning process of students and students get more insight into their own development.

Instruments such as these that ensure that students basically administer themselves (by scheduling interviews themselves, by entering a record of feedback dialogues themselves, etc.) fit well within the high impact learning approach because they also primarily encourage learner agency (self-management).

DOI: 10.4324/9781003294139-28

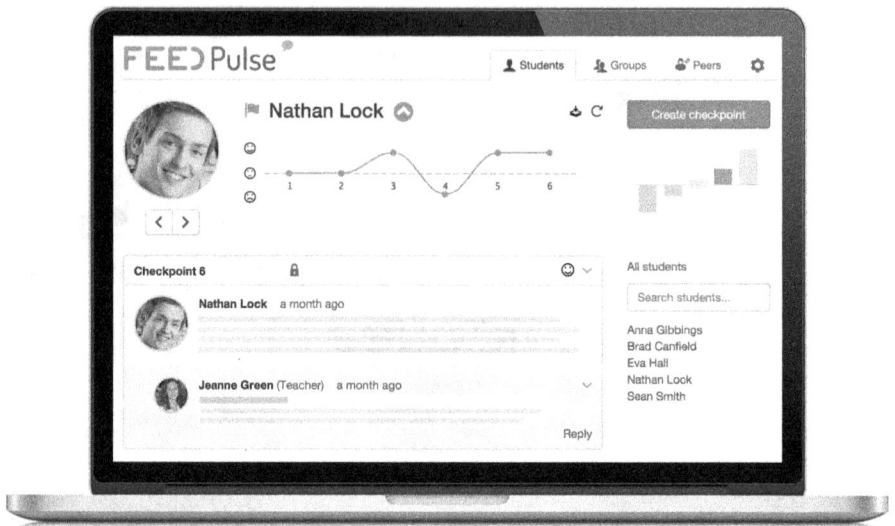

Figure 23.1 FeedPulse Global View.

The software easily allows the creation of checkpoints: moments for a feedback dialogue (see Figure 23.2). After the dialogue, a report can easily be made and viewed by the parties to whom access is granted. If desired, an expert can check whether the feedback was properly understood.

Frank Haverkort says: *Within our training programme, students are provided with developmental feedback at multiple times. FeedPulse (LTI application integrated into Canvas) is used within many educational units to support the feedback process. Unambiguous use of FeedPulse within the institute is very important for the student.*

Students at the Eindhoven IT programme are provided with development-oriented feedback on their overall performance at several moments. The various measurement moments are learning moments for the student (and teacher) and can provide valuable information about the development (on the various learning outcomes). Students themselves process the feedback they receive in dialogue in FeedPulse at a 'checkpoint'. This activates them and makes them partly responsible for their own development. Because the feedback from multiple measurement moments can be recorded in the tool, an overview of the students' development over time is created. This makes it easy for the teacher to monitor the students' learning process and students gain more insight into their own development. All feedback given, products delivered and reviews of these can ultimately form the basis for the integral final assessment (Assessment-as-Learning). If all goes well, this will no longer be a surprise for the student.

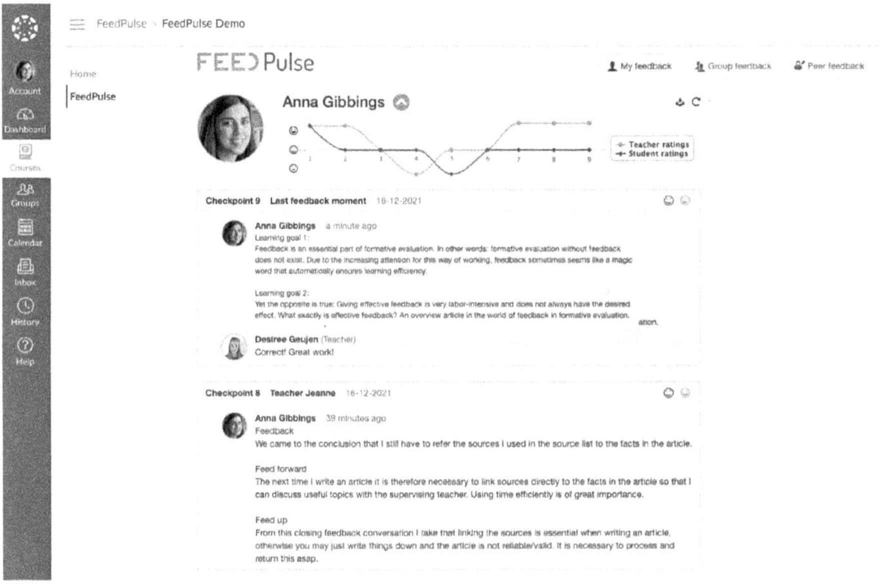

Figure 23.2 FeedPulse feedback dialogue moments.

Functions

Checkpoint

A checkpoint stands for a measurement moment/feedback moment. The teacher creates a checkpoint for a student or group of students at the moment the feedback is given. The student writes down the feedback received in the checkpoint.

Possible help questions for students when describing the feedback in a checkpoint:

- *What went well?*
- *What should you pay more attention to?*
- *What is your next step towards achieving the learning outcomes?*

Smiley rating

At a checkpoint, the teacher gives a rating of the student's overall performance (in relation to the learning outcomes) by means of a smiley rating. The graph in Figure 23.3 illustrates this.

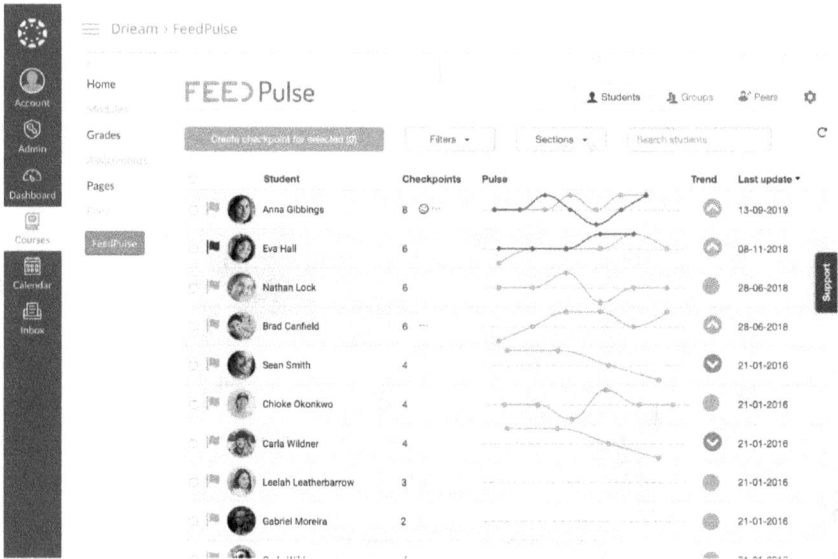

Figure 23.3 Guideline for smiley rating at checkpoints by the teacher as an appreciation of student performance.

Explanation of the meaning of smileys:

- *You show something special and are good at demonstrating the learning outcome (above expectations).*
- *You have shown something good and are well on your way to demonstrating the learning outcomes.*
- *You have not shown anything or anything that is not good enough. You really have to go the extra mile to demonstrate the learning outcome.*

Optional self-rating

In order to involve the student even more in the feedback process and to make him think about his own development, the student can (optionally) also give himself a rating at a checkpoint. Possible differences in self-rating and teacher-rating can be valuable input for the feedback discussion.

Peers

Peers can be turned on via the settings menu. An extra tab appears. The student can give feedback to fellow students in the group, several times over time.

Way of working with FeedPulse within Fontys ICT

For students it is nice if all lecturers who use FeedPulse do this in the same way as much as possible, so that students get used to a uniform way of working. The use of FeedPulse within Fontys ICT is described in steps as below. This process also applies to the use of FeedPulse in project groups. The teacher gives regular oral feedback, feed-up and feedforward to the project group. One student of the group fills in the feedback, the other group members can respond if necessary.

1. The teacher or students create a checkpoint.
2. The teacher and students sit together and verbal feedback, feed-up and feedforward are exchanged and discussed about the overall performance regarding the learning outcomes. You can also use the help questions for this.
3. The student notes down the feedback, feed-up and feedforward in FeedPulse during the discussion. Notes may also be made and elaborated on later.
4. The teacher gives a smiley rating on the overall performance of the student at that moment immediately after the discussion.
5. The next feedback moment (e.g. one or two weeks later), the student looks back on the previous feedback moment (previous checkpoint). How is the student's performance now? And what has been done with the feedback, feed-up and feedforward from last time?
6. The teacher creates a new checkpoint and has the student type in the feedback, feed-up and feedforward at this new checkpoint.

Practical points for the teacher

- When you give a negative smiley, do check what the student has written down and whether he understands why it is still insufficient. If the student is not present or does not communicate sufficiently, you can give a negative smiley without the student having written down feedback.
- The smiley rating indicates how you value the overall performance of the student at that moment. It is not necessary to improve or complete the written down feedback of the student at every checkpoint. However, you can do this if it helps to better secure the feedback in FeedPulse.
- Answering a question does not require FeedPulse to be completed.

Figure 23.4 shows the example of working with FeedPulse.

Figure 23.4 Example of working with FeedPulse.

GrowFlow (GrowFlow app)

GrowFlow by Shareworks is an online learning tool that stimulates learner agency in a structured way. Students are given responsibility for their own learning goals and their own learning process. This tool also originated from practice, especially the SEAL project in which Jos Speetjens and Annemarie Van den Broek played a significant role, together with Dries van de Enden in the development of GrowFlow.

All variants of high impact learning use many authentic projects. Students learn a lot as a result. However, for coaches it is a challenge to assess whether all learning goals have been achieved for a group and for each individual student.

GrowFlow solves this by placing more responsibilities with the student. Students keep track of their own actions, feedback and learning goals. Coaches see the results during coach meetings for discussion. This makes the learning process more effective and more exciting for students and coaches.

Coaches can thus create learner groups (Figure 23.5) and students can then add their actions and feedback during a project (Figure 23.6 and 23.7).

During the learning process, students can oversee all actions in various dashboards (Figure 23.8).

Students do indeed personalise their own learning goals (Figure 23.9) and add their own actions (Figure 23.10).

GrowFlow uses continuous peer feedback. By logging all their actions directly and reflecting using peer feedback, students learn more. The data-rich dashboards serve two functions: student reflection and structuring team meetings with coaches. All data can also be easily exported. GrowFlow is above all mobile-friendly. Students can easily add actions and

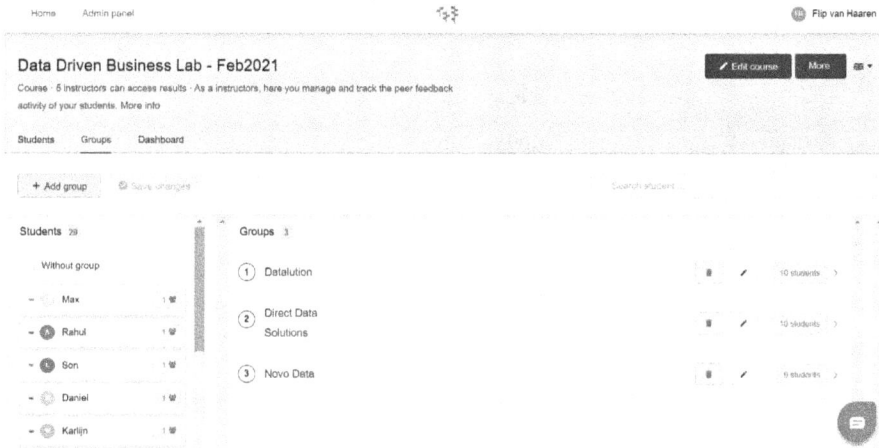

Figure 23.5 Creating learner groups in GrowFlow.

give feedback to group members from their smartphone. GrowFlow can either be added to your learning management systems (LMS) or you can use it as a standalone web application.

Jos Speetjens: *In environments where group learning is more central, the role of peers becomes more important. Peers provide feedback on both process and self-regulation. The GrowFlow tool supports this process. The learner takes the initiative to request feedback from peers by entering actions taken based on learning*

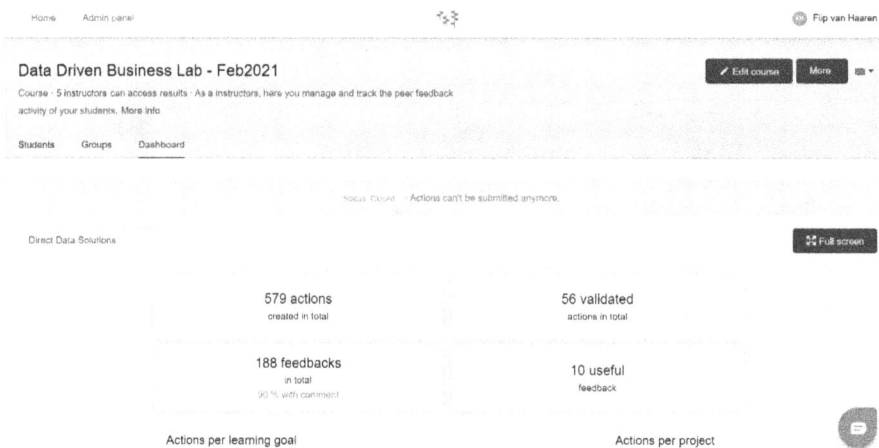

Figure 23.6 Example of a course/project and student actions and feedback overview.

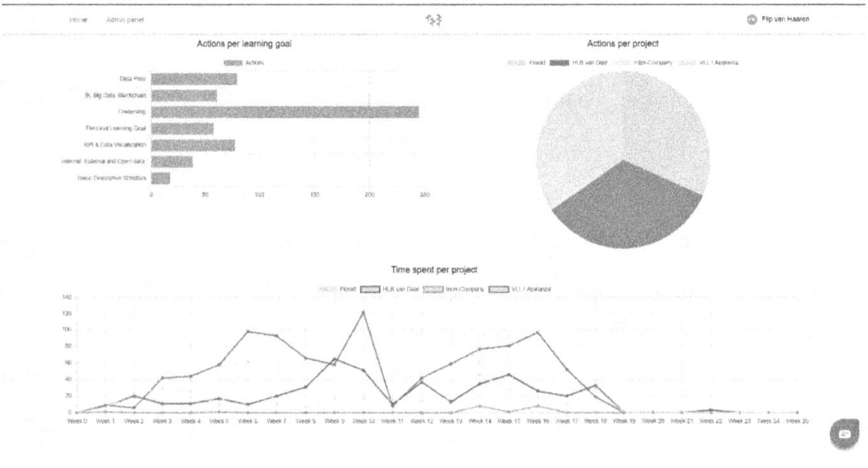

Figure 23.7 Overview on actions per goal and per project.

outcomes (learning objectives or competencies). The peers give feedback on these actions and indicate what they think the impact of the action was on the progress of the group process. In the ensuing conversation, the meaning, strength and depth of the feedback is discussed with the facilitator and the peers together. The system is supportive in that this is visible to all involved at that moment. All learners themselves give meaning to the feedback and formulate possible improvements to both the behaviour and the feedback.

Jos Speetjens: *In GrowFlow, the leading action comes from the student himself in combination with the peers. The feedback dialogue is central here: meaning is given*

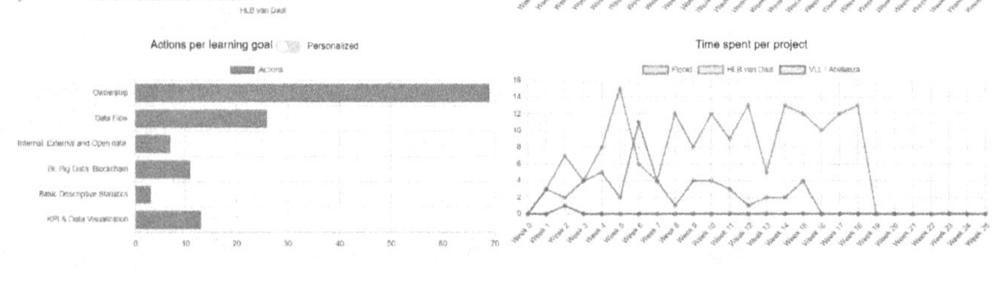

Figure 23.8 A GrowFlow dashboard.

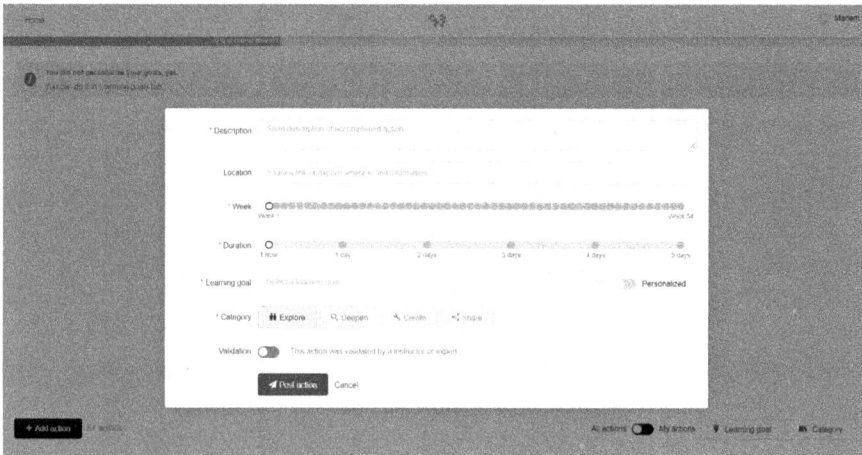

Figure 23.9 Personalising your own learning goals.

in face-to-face contact between parties. In the absence of that contact, GrowFlow quickly becomes empty or polluted by superficial and meaningless feedback.

Egodact challenge monitor and progress monitor

One of the high impact learning variants is challenge-based learning (Dochy, Berghmans, Koenen, & Segers, 2016; Dochy, Segers, & Messmann, 2018; Dochy, Gijbels, Segers, & Van den Bossche 2020). More and more learning

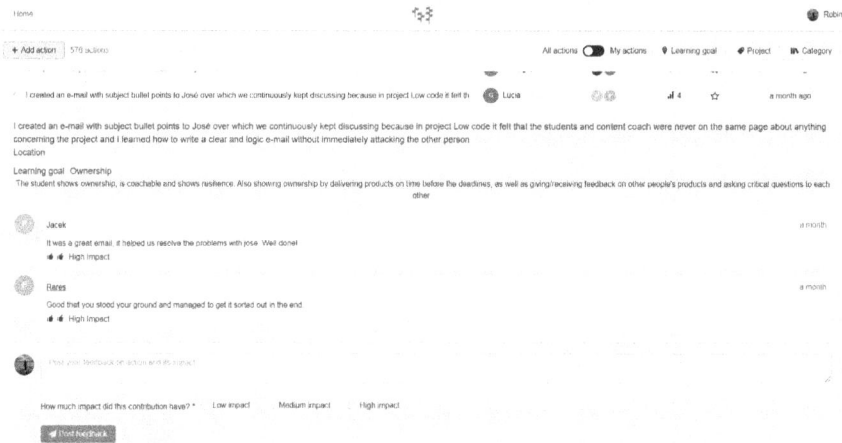

Figure 23.10 Adding your own actions.

hubs that support their learning processes by starting from learners' own challenges use the Egodact challenge monitor and progress monitor.

In the challenge monitor, students keep a portfolio of their projects/ challenges via a Kanban board. Students always go through the same process, and in this way, they can work on their project independently.

The Egodact Challenge Monitor consists of a Kanban board: rows, each of which is divided into three columns: to do, in progress and done (see Figure 23.11). A row is an umbrella topic under which challenges can be grouped. These challenges can be dragged and dropped into the different columns.

In addition, learners go through various steps for each challenge they tackle individually or in teams and keep track of their key competences. Here, feedback dialogues with the learning coach and feedback from peers play a crucial role.

Griet Mertens (Learning hub De Met): *The only time we sometimes give written feedback (and thus in the margin of the feedback from the coach) is when we go through the challenge monitor in the evening and discover that a student has not filled in any goals for a new challenge, for example. Then we write a little catcall so that the student can see this immediately the next day when he starts (there will be a blue dot next to the challenge so he sees that there is feedback). We notice that such very targeted feedback works.*

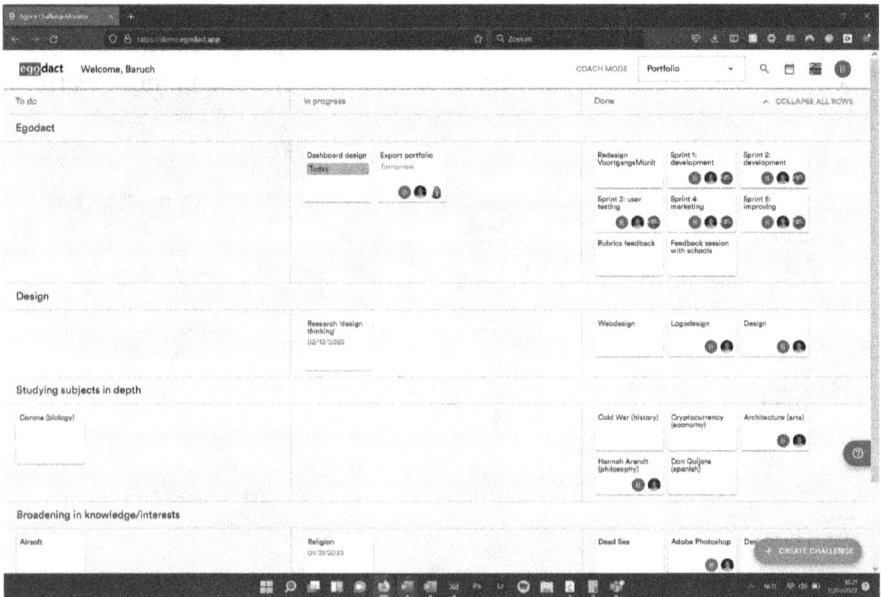

Figure 23.11 A Kanban board.

The progress monitor gives students an overview of rubrics (provided by the coach/school) in which they can record their progress autonomously and proactively (see Figure 23.12 and 23.13).

The coach confirms or refutes this progress only on the basis of a feedback dialogue or a coach discussion. Sliders have also been added: through their colours, they show the student's progress within the levels of the rubric (see Figure 23.14).

Using the slider below the levels, students can indicate their progress as owners of their own development. The plus buttons can be used to add a link (e.g. a link to a challenge from the Challenge Monitor or a link to a product) to that level which serves as proof that that level has actually been reached. Pupils move the blue bar to indicate their progress. The purple bar is moved by the learning coach after the feedback session in consultation with the learner. The learner then always understands exactly why the purple bar is set at a particular level.

Griet Mertens (Learning hub De Met) about this: *With* reflection *and with the bars it works as follows. We ask the students to fill these in independently before the coaching session and to take their time for this so that there is time during the coaching session to discuss them together and to add to them if necessary. The student sets the bars for the coaching session, the coach completes them during the*

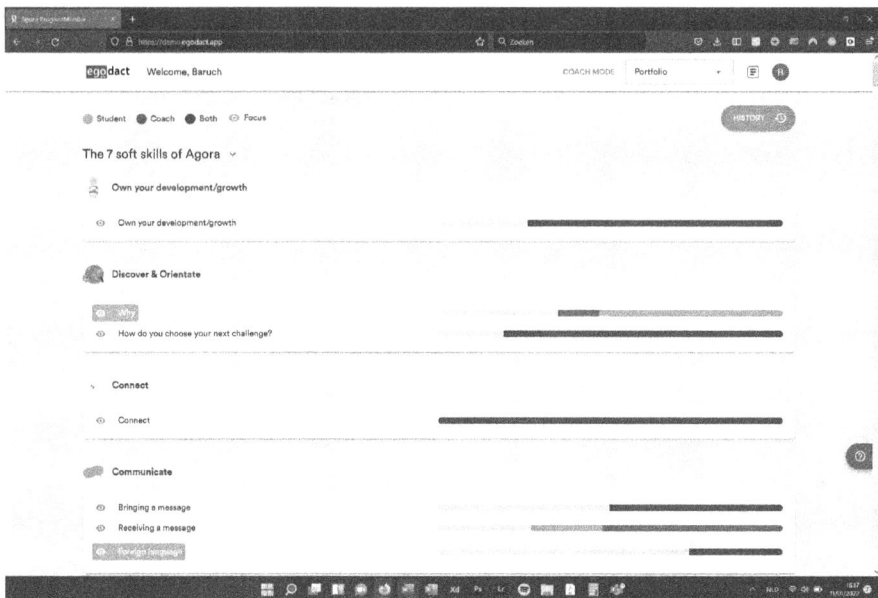

Figure 23.12 The progress monitor 1.

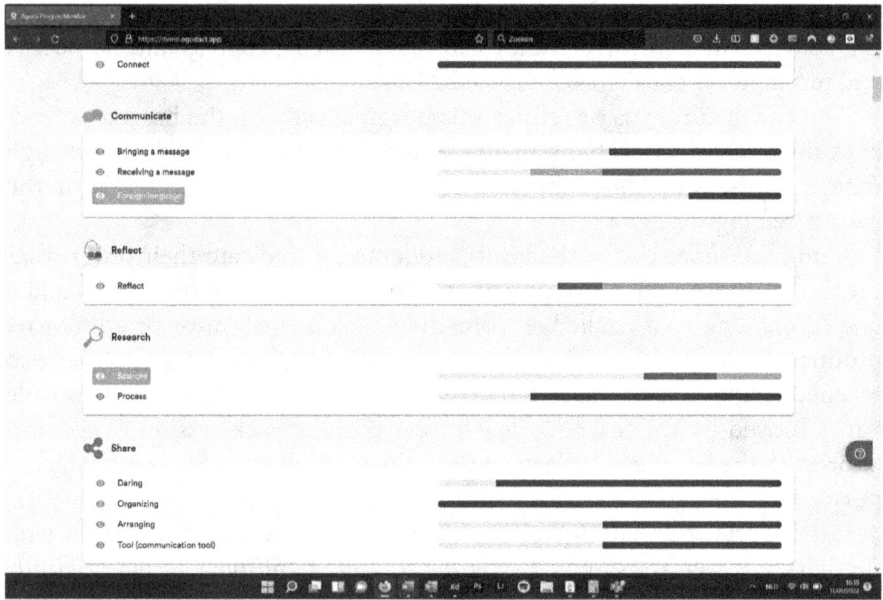

Figure 23.13 The progress monitor 2.

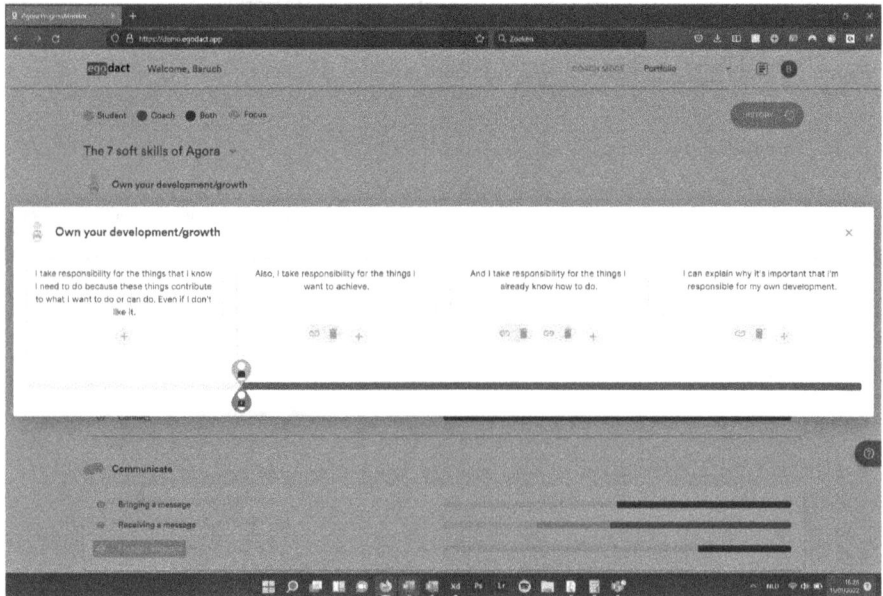

Figure 23.14 Sliders used in the progress monitor.

coaching session in consultation with the student. They then look at the preview together in order to consciously take one or two missions to the next challenge.

The progress monitor builds on intrinsic motivation. This was initially done by replacing grades with rubrics that comprehensively describe all levels within a section. This way it is always clear what a level achieved within a section means. This clarity contributes to motivation and stimulates ownership of development. Second, the monitor contributes to Assessment-as-Learning by focusing on the development of the individual. Moreover, students gain insight into what is going well and what can be improved. This also leads to intrinsic motivation and ownership of their own development and growth. Assessment-as-Learning stimulates real learning and making mistakes is allowed.

In addition, strong PCP coaching is of great importance. A learning coach ensures that the learner really gets going and that intrinsic motivation really comes through. This means that they especially stimulate and monitor. This stimulation can be done by asking questions and creating awareness: 'How can these rubrics help you grow?'

Friday feedback

Friday feedback is an online web-based platform designed for small-to-medium-sized organisations that uses real-time insights to stimulate and optimise organisational communication and employee engagement. Therefore, while this is intended for business managers, training managers and education managers can also benefit from it. The tool can certainly be used as input for weekly feedback dialogues.

The software provides people managers with a platform to gather consistent, honest feedback from learners or employees, maintain a happy team and improve employee retention.

Through regular check-in surveys with learners or employees (see Figure 23.15), Friday feedback enables managers to uncover problems, discover opportunities and maintain a happy, productive work team. The quick surveys – which include '1–10 scales' and free-response questions – encourage learners or employees to leave constructive, concise feedback for managers (see Figure 23.16). This eliminates guesswork for managers about how learners or employees are feeling and provides them with immediate, interpretable feedback. Based on the survey results, Friday feedback generates a 'Team Happiness Index' – a weekly, measurable picture of learner or staff satisfaction, in itself a very simple but nice input for the weekly feedback dialogue with the teams or individuals.

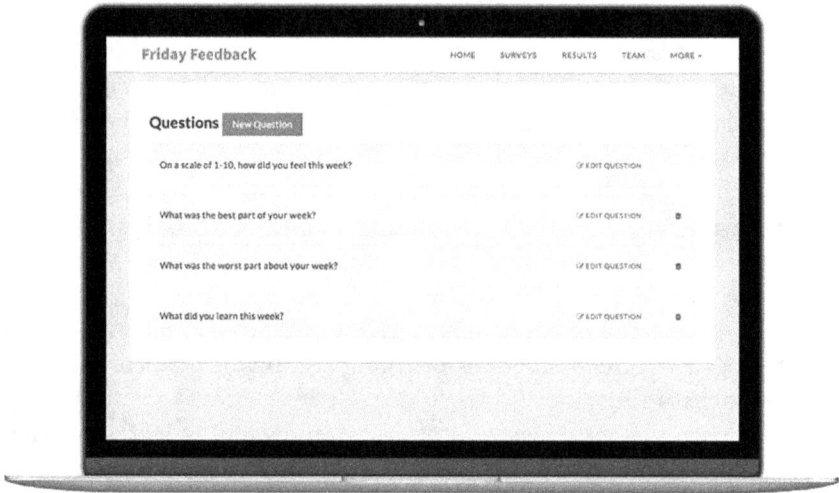

Figure 23.15 Example questions in Friday Feedback.

FeedbackFruits

FeedbackFruits Tool Suite from G2 was born out of a desire to encourage interaction between students and lecturers. Lectures have long been a one-way system for delivering information, with little opportunity for student engagement. Overcoming this obstacle is central to the company's mission:

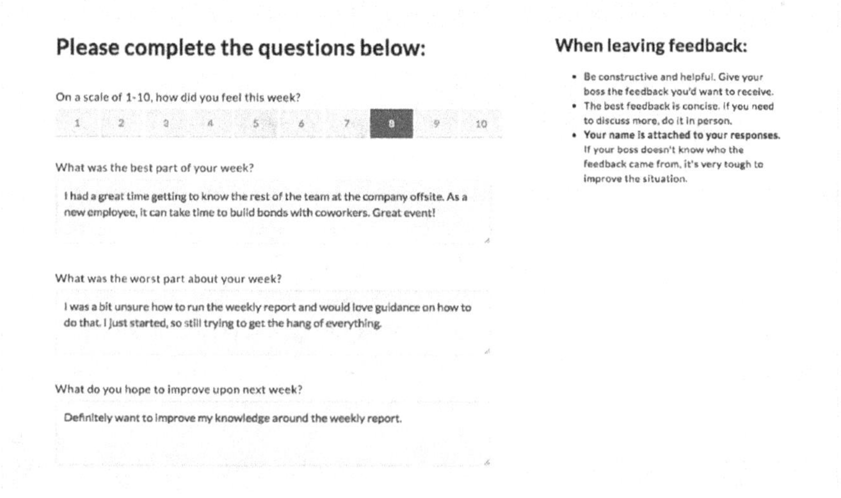

Figure 23.16 Examples of feedback in Friday Feedback.

helping lecturers develop engaging learning activities. FeedbackFruits has developed a suite of pedagogical tools that can be integrated into LMSs to give educators extensive capabilities in designing courses and improving the quality of the student learning experience. The package is very feature-rich and the tools are constantly being updated and modified.

There are undoubtedly advantages to this package such as integration of interactive audio and interactive video, peer review of papers and so on. However, there are also clear potential disadvantages to this package.

For one thing, it can do a lot (perhaps too much), which means that as a user you will only use a very small part of it. Compare this with the 90 apps on your mobile phone, only a few of which you use.

On the other hand, it is clear that the structure of this package is based on traditional education that works with lectures (think for example of the interactive questions that you can add to PowerPoint slides), lessons in classes and with many tests. You can try to pimp that, but the question is whether it really works. The question is then how to achieve learner agency and urgency. In any case, it is clear that the package offers support for lectures, for knowledge tests, and emphasises anonymity of feedback and test results, for example. These are all aspects that we want to avoid in future-oriented training. After reading this book, this will be clear to you.

Because there are so many updates and new features in the pipeline, it is rather unclear what new features will be worked on. Most potential users do not have the time to follow this up.

Examples of learning activities are the following: Students review each other's draft group reports before final submission, students provide feedback on their peers' collaboration skills so that instructors discover free riders in group projects, instructor evaluates student assignments or classroom presentations according to his/her own rubric and students receive AI-driven instant feedback on their written work.

Such automated feedback also leads to doubts, since we know from research that written feedback often has very little effect and that feedback that is not based on dialogue, that is mainly one-way, directed, not necessarily understood and not linked to an action plan, has little effect. One does try to generate a dialogue with peers, but in a traditional educational context, the question is how well this can work. This is done by giving explicit instructions, whereby one can wonder whether this is not too steering for the student of tomorrow.

In short, FeedbackFruits is a very extensive software package with a lot of potential. Hopefully, FeedbackFruits will soon join in with the new developments such as Assessment-as-Learning, more learner agency and working from a real sense of urgency and intrinsic motivation.

Simple feedback tools   **24**

There are many simple feedback tools that are easy to print and can do a lot of service in any training room. Several of the boxes we have already presented in this book can fulfil this function, but also other simple feedback tools can do that. Hanging them in every corner of every classroom can make a difference because then every team that enters a feedback dialogue in a corner can use them.

De MET feedback tool

Together with the learning coaches of the Met learning hubs (see earlier), we developed a feedback framework for the dialogical feedback between learning coach and learners (Figure 24.1), as well as for the feedback that learners expect in response to their presentations (Figure 24.2). These can be found schematically below.

DOI: 10.4324/9781003294139-29

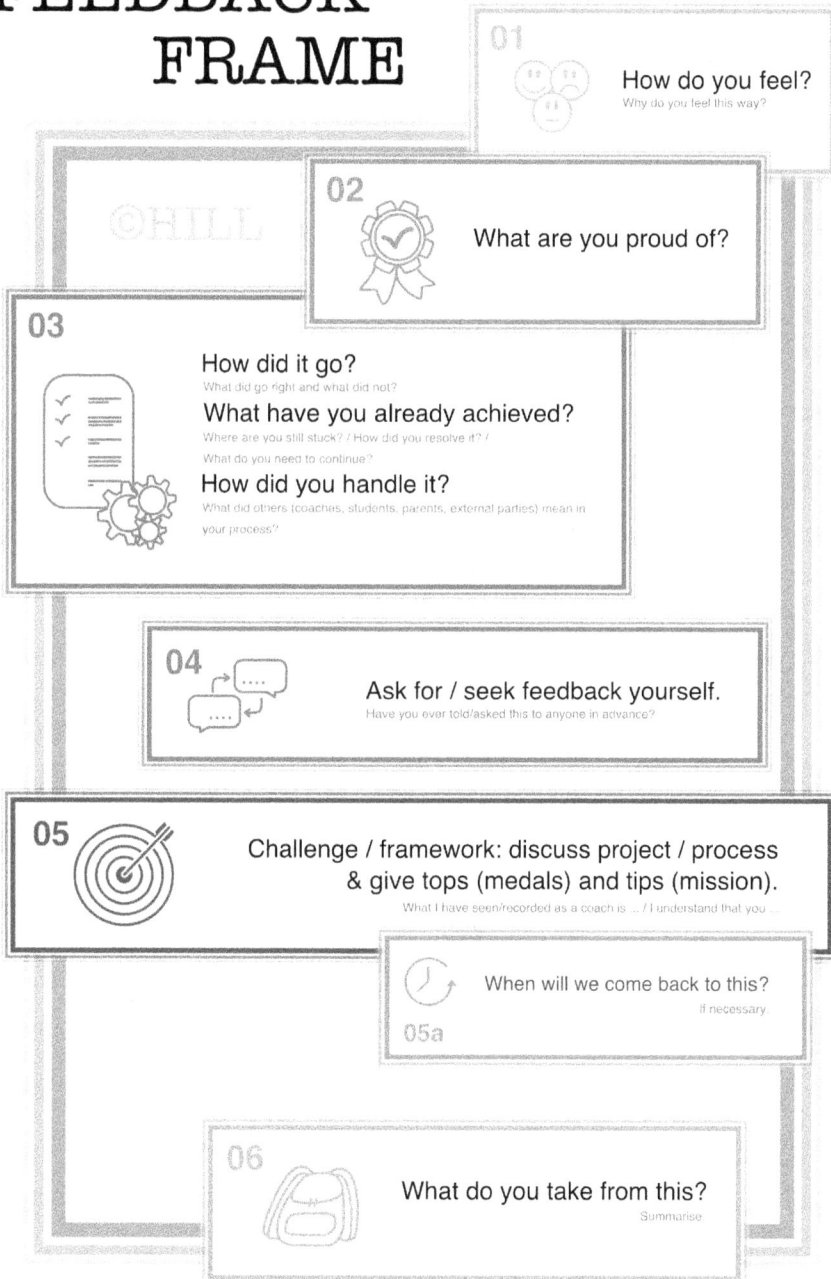

FEEDBACK FRAME

01 How do you feel?
Why do you feel this way?

02 What are you proud of?

03
How did it go?
What did go right and what did not?
What have you already achieved?
Where are you still stuck? / How did you resolve it? /
What do you need to continue?
How did you handle it?
What did others (coaches, students, parents, external parties) mean in
your process?

04 Ask for / seek feedback yourself.
Have you ever told/asked this to anyone in advance?

05 Challenge / framework: discuss project / process
& give tops (medals) and tips (mission).
What I have seen/recorded as a coach is ... / I understand that you ...

05a When will we come back to this?
If necessary

06 What do you take from this?
Summarise

Figure 24.1 Feedback framework for the dialogic feedback between learning coach and learners.

Plenary feedback in the learning group

a. **Questions to the presenter**
   1. What was it like for you to give this presentation (let off steam)?
   2. If you were to do it again, what would you keep and what would you do differently?

b. **Questions for the audience**
   1. *Learning coach summarises what student says*/Do you agree with this feedback? What do you recognise and what don't you recognise? Additions? *(first positive, then mission)*?
   2. *Presenter:* Summarise what you take away from this?
   3. *Listeners:* What do you take away from this presentation?
   4. *Listeners:* What made you remember this, what did you need to remember even more?
   5. *Presenter:* Have you been able to reach everyone? For example, a glossary/information given out in advance.

c. **Individual feedback to the presenter**
   1. What do you remember from the audience's feedback? Can you summarise?
   2. What have others (persons and sources), coaches, pupils, parents and external parties meant in your process?
   3. What was it like for you to give this presentation to this group? How do you think you can take your presentation to the next level? Do you feel you have reached everyone? Had you thoroughly checked the initial situation of the group?
   4. Are there any questions from this presentation that you would like to work on further?

TIP for the coaches:
   Content! What do you remember from the presentation you just saw?
   How do you anchor the content? For example, by a reading assignment, case study, search, activating prior knowledge, coaching the students to → How are you going to do the presentation so that others also learn a lot from it?

Figure 24.2 Feedback framework for feedback on presentations.

Continue with feedback dialogues

How?

Feedback dialogues are the beating heart of learning with impact

Learning with impact is intrinsically motivated. That is why Assessment-as-Learning is the way forward. The most important thing is that we change our habits as coaches of learning processes in such a way that feedback becomes the core activity of learning, because we have known for a long time that feedback moments are the moments when learners really acquire expertise. In addition, feedback can only become a core activity if it is embedded in dialogue; that is the beating heart of high-impact learning.

Feedback dialogues are crucial for Assessment-as-Learning

Giving scores to learners, or making red flags in a paper, or giving short written comments on a test or a piece of work are all very weak forms of feedback with very little impact. Especially since they do not build up trust, nor do they provide a mutual expression of deep understanding and exchange of that understanding. Therefore, they do not contribute to the required mindset that is essential for feedback to have the necessary impact. Assessment-as-Learning is the continuous exchange of feedback in a dialogue on a weekly basis. In this way, we stimulate and facilitate an attitude of seeking feedback that leads learners to learner agency. This is the way to increase impact.

DOI: 10.4324/9781003294139-30

Feedback dialogues are the core of PCP coaching

Having a learning coach who will monitor you as a learning partner based on constructive feedback and trust speeds up the way forward.

Our high-impact learning that lasts model also encourages asking learners to self-document the feedback they receive. This reduces a potential administrative burden on learning coaches, sets a standard for learner agency and ensures that learners take responsibility for monitoring their own process. Of course, a HILL mindset is needed in the learner group to establish this habit and of course also in the team of learning coaches. An in-depth professionalisation trajectory aimed at progress-oriented, content-oriented and process-oriented (PCP) coaching during feedback dialogues is not a luxury.

The High-Impact Learning Academy will be happy to help you overcome these hurdles towards the learning of the future (www.highimpactlearningthatlasts.com). The underlying mechanism of high-impact learning that lasts, feedback dialogues, Assessment-as-Learning and PCP coaching has emerged not only from many scientific studies but also from the co-construction, discussion, consultation between us as authors and scientists who came up with the core of 'expansive learning' and 3G assessment. Our conversations (FtF and online) with Mary James (Cambridge) and Yrjö Engeström (Helsinki) sparked an interaction of thought streams on the 'theory of expansive learning' linked to Assessment-as-Learning and 3G assessment. There was also an interesting line of interaction between us and the various practitioners/researchers who described their practices in Part 3. This seems to us an instructive way of evaluating a learning theory that is adapted to the practice of learning in a society that will change exponentially in the near future. After all, learning with impact is dialogue.

Finally, we are currently conducting a study that will be published soon. The study overviews the effects of high-impact learning practices (Arikan, Dochy, & Segers, 2022). As a result of this review, 127 unique articles were reached and after the inclusion criteria were applied, 56 articles were found suitable for this review. As a result of the detailed review, in 12 articles, the Assessment-as-Learning building blocks of the HILL model are defined as one of the key elements explaining the effects of high-impact learning practices. In the articles reviewed, it was highlighted that constructive, timely and frequent feedback improves students' self-regulation habits (Weber & Myrick, 2018) and provides students with the opportunity to combine, synthesise and apply what they have learned (Cotten & Thompson, 2017). Additionally, it was mentioned that while it increases students' self-confidence and motivation, it reduces students' stress (Ishaq & Bass, 2019).

Weber and Myrick (2018) emphasised that not only the feedback given by a coach but also the peer-to-peer feedback provides students useful information and new perspectives. And as said in our introductory part, feedback becomes more powerful when feedback seeking and feedback dialogues come into play.

Nevertheless, change and educational innovation does not happen in a vacuum but is an integral part of an environment where learners are supported to develop their talents. What are the features or building blocks of an environment where feedback dialogues can play fully their powerful role? Of course, feedback dialogues cannot force the change on their own. According to the results obtained from the research, the collaboration and coaching, learner agency and urgency are the other HILL model building blocks that are needed to construct the required learning environment. Forty six out of 56 articles stated that the collaboration and coaching plays a crucial role in the success of high-impact learning practices. Through collaboration and coaching, students learn to work together effectively (Einbinder, 2018), have the opportunity to brainstorm, develop materials, learn from each other's experiences (Anderson, Boyd, Marin, & McNamara, 2019) and gain new perspectives while re-evaluating their old perspectives (Bonet & Walters, 2016). Furthermore, the positive effects of the learner agency on student learning were emphasised in 30 articles. According to them, learner agency improves students' analytical and critical thinking (Einbinder, 2018; Miller, Rycek, & Fritson, 2011), leadership skills (Bampasidou, Grogan, Clark, & Sandberg, 2016), awareness personal values and beliefs (Cotten & Thompson, 2017), problem solving skills (Armstrong-Mensah, Ramsey-White, & Alema-Mensah, 2019) and self-efficacy (Cotten & Thompson, 2017). In addition, 21 articles mentioned the positive effects of urgency on student learning. As it was mentioned in these studies, high-impact learning practices provide students with job-related knowledge and skills for their future careers (Armstrong-Mensah et al., 2019; Bampasidou et al., 2016) and prepare graduates for employment after graduation with real-life experiences (Murphrey, Odom, & Sledd, 2016), they attract students' attention and make their learning more meaningful.

Additionally, as a result of our research, it was found that high-impact learning practices have 18 different positive effects in practice. High-impact learning practices not only make learning more meaningful as they allow students to apply what they have learned and prepare them for their future careers (Bampasidou et al., 2016; Murphrey et al., 2016) but also provide transformative learning as they give students the ability to bridge the knowledge and skills gained during their university education (Zilvinskis & Dumford, 2018). In addition, thanks to the projects, they provide learning in and out of the classroom (Armstrong-Mensah et al., 2019). Moreover, high-impact practices promote student engagement, graduation rates and GPA (Armstrong-Mensah et al., 2019; Myers, Myers, & Peters, 2019; Murphrey et al.), increase both students' academic success and motivation (Miller et al., 2011), support personal and social development (Miller et al., 2011), enhance leadership skills (Bampasidou et al., 2016), make students willing to be tolerant of different points of views (Myers et al., 2019) and promote student-faculty/peer/community interaction (Armstrong-Mensah et al., 2019). In addition, students who participate in high-impact learning practices learn to think critically and analytically (Myers et al., 2019), manage time (Bampasidou et al., 2016), take responsibility for their own learning and become aware of their own abilities, skills and beliefs (Goulette & Denney, 2018).

Convinced to go all the way?

References

Adalberon, E. (2021). Providing assessment feedback to pre-service teachers: A study of examiners' comments. *Assessment & Evaluation in Higher Education*, 46(4), 601–614.

Adams, S. M. (2005). Positive affect and feedback-giving behavior. *Journal of Managerial Psychology*, 20(1), 24–42.

Ajjawi, R., & Boud, D. (2018). Examining the nature and effects of feedback dialogue. *Assessment & Evaluation in Higher Education*, 43(7), 1106–1119.

Alkaher, I., & Dolan, E. (2011). Instructors' decisions that integrate inquiry teaching into undergraduate courses: How do I make this fit? *International Journal of Teaching and Learning*, 5, 1–24.

Amah, O. E. (2008). Feedback management strategies in perceived good and poor performance: The role of source attributes and recipient's personality disposition. *Research and Practice in Human Resource Management*, 16(1), 39–59.

Anderson, K. L., Boyd, M., Ariemma Marin, K., & McNamara, K. (2019). Reimagining service-learning: Deepening the impact of this high-impact practice. *Journal of Experiential Education*, 42(3), 229–248.

Andrade, H. L. (2019). A critical review of research on student self-assessment. *Frontiers in Education*, 4(3), 87.

Anseel, F., & Brutus, S. (2019). Checking in? A dyadic and dynamic perspective on feedback conversations. Feedback at work (pp. 29–51). Cham: Springer.

Anseel, F., Lievens, F., & Levy, P. E. (2007). A self-motives perspective on feedback-seeking behavior: Linking organizational behavior and social psychology research. *International Journal of Management Reviews*, 9(3), 211–236.

Anseel, F., Lievens, F., & Schollaert, E. (2009). Reflection as a strategy to enhance task performance after feedback. *Organizational Behavior and Human Decision Processes*, 110(1), 23–35.

Anseel, F., Vossaert, L., & Corneillie, E. (2018). Like ships passing in the night: toward a truly dyadic perspective on feedback dynamics. *Management Research: Journal of the Iberoamerican Academy of Management*, 16(4), 334 -342. https://doi. org/10.1108/MRJIAM-12-2017-0794

Anseel, F., Beatty, A. S., Shen, W., Lievens, F., & Sackett, P. R. (2015). How are we doing after 30 years? A meta-analytic review of the antecedents and outcomes of feedback-seeking behavior. *Journal of Management*, 41(1), 318–348.

Arikan, S., Dochy, F., & Segers, M. (2022). What effects do high impact learning practices have? A review study in higher education. *Educational Research Review* (submitted).

Armstrong-Mensah, E., Ramsey-White, K., & Alema-Mensah, E. (2019). Integrative learning in US undergraduate public health education: A review of student perceptions of effective high-impact educational practices at Georgia State University. *Frontiers in Public Health*, 7, 101.

Ashford, S. J. (1986). Feedback-seeking in individual adaptation: A resource perspective. *Academy of Management Journal*, 29(3), 465–487.

Ashford, S. J., & Cummings, L. L. (1983). Feedback as an individual resource: Personal strategies of creating information. *Organizational Behavior and Human Performance*, 32(3), 370–398.

Ashford, S. J., & Northcraft, G. B. (1992). Conveying more (or less) than we realize: The role of impression-management in feedback-seeking. *Organizational Behavior and Human Decision Processes*, 53(3), 310–334.

Ashford, S. J., & Tsui, A. S. (1991). Self-regulation for managerial effectiveness: The role of active feedback seeking. *Academy of Management Journal*, 34(2), 251–280.

Ashford, S. J., Blatt, R., & VandeWalle, D. (2003). Reflections on the looking glass: A review of research on feedback-seeking behavior in organizations. *Journal of Management*, 29(6), 773–799.

Ashford, S. J., De Stobbeleir, K., & Nujella, M. (2016). To seek or not to seek: Is that the only question? Recent developments in feedback-seeking literature. *Annual Review of Organizational Psychology and Organizational Behavior*, 3, 213–239.

Baartman, L., van Schilt-Mol, T., & Van der Vleuten, C. (2020). Programmatisch toetsen: Voorbeelden. Amsterdam: Boom.

Ballantyne, R., Hughes, K., & Mylonas, A. (2002). Developing procedures for implementing peer assessment in large classes using an action research process. *Assessment & Evaluation in Higher Education*, 27, 427–441. doi:10.1080/0260293022000009302

Bampasidou, M., Grogan, K., Clark, J., & Sandberg, M. (2016). Career skills: Perceptions of importance and high impact learning activities for skill development in agricultural economics and agribusiness programs 1. *NACTA Journal*, 60(1a), 36.

Baron, R. A. (1988). Negative effects of destructive criticism: Impact on conflict, self-efficacy, and task performance. *Journal of Applied Psychology*, 73(2), 199.

Bangert-Drowns, R. L., Kulik, C.-L. C., Kulik, J. A., & Morgan, M. (1991). The instructional effect of feedback in test-like events. *Review of Educational Research*, 61, 213–238.

Belschak, F. D., & Den Hartog, D. N. (2009). Consequences of positive and negative feedback: The impact on emotions and extra-role behaviors. *Applied Psychology*, 58(2), 274–303.

Birenbaum, M. (1996). Assessment 2000: Towards a pluralistic approach to assessment. In M. Birenbaum, & F. Dochy, (Eds.). Alternatives in assessment of achievements, learning processes and prior knowledge (Vol. 42). Dordrecht: Springer Science & Business Media.

Birenbaum, M., & Dochy, F. (Eds.). (1996). Alternatives in assessment of achievements, learning processes and prior knowledge (Vol. 42). New York: Springer Science & Business Media, LLC.

Black, P., & McCormick, R. (2010). Reflections and new directions. *Assessment & Evaluation in Higher Education*, 35, 493–499. doi:10.1080/02602938.2010.493696

Black, P., & William, D. (1998). Assessment and classroom learning. *Assessment in Education: Principles, Policy and Practice*, 5, 7–73. doi:10.1080/0969595980050102

Black, P., & Wiliam, D. (2005). Developing a theory of formative assessment. In J. Gardner (Ed.), Assessment and learning (pp. 81–100). London: Sage.

Blair, A., & McGinty, S. (2013). Feedback-dialogues: Exploring the student perspective. *Assessment & Evaluation in Higher Education*, 38(4), 466–476, doi:10.1080/02602938.2011.649244

Bloxham, S., & Campbell, L. (2010). Generating dialogue in assessment feedback: Exploring the use of interactive cover sheet. *Assessment & Evaluation in Higher Education*, 35, 291–300. doi:10.1080/02602931003650045

Brooks, C., Carroll, A., Gillies, R. M., & Hattie, J. (2019). A Matrix of Feedback for Learning. *Australian Journal of Teacher Education*, 44(4). http://dx.doi.org/10.14221/ajte.2018v44n4.2.

Bolzer, M., Strijbos, J. W., & Fischer, F. (2015). Inferring mindful cognitive-processing of peer-feedback via eye-tracking: Role of feedback-characteristics, fixation-durations and transitions. *Journal of Computer Assisted Learning*, 31(5), 422–434.

Bonet, G., & Walters, B. R. (2016). High impact practices: Student engagement and retention. *College Student Journal*, 50(2), 224–235.

Borgatti, S. P., & Cross, R. (2003). A relational view of information seeking and learning in social networks. *Management Science*, 49(4), 432–445.

Boud, D., & Falchikov, N. (Eds.). (2007). Rethinking assessment in higher education. Oxford, UK: Routledge.

Brearley, F., & Cullen, W. (2012). Providing students with formative audio feedback. *Bioscience Education*, 20(1), 22–36.

Brinko, K. T. (1993). The practice of giving feedback to improve teaching: What is effective? *The Journal of Higher Education*, 64(5), 574–593.

Brookhart, S. M., & Chen, F. (2015). The quality and effectiveness of descriptive rubrics. *Educational Review, 67*(3), 343–368.

Burke, R. J., Weitzel, W., & Weir, T. (1978). Characteristics of effective employee performance review and development interviews: Replication and extension 1. *Personnel Psychology, 31*(4), 903–919.

Butler, L. B., & Winne, P. H. (1995). Feedback and self-regulated learning: A theoretical synthesis. *Review of Educational Research, 65,* 245–281.

Carless, D. (2006). Differing perceptions in the feedback process. *Studies in Higher Education, 31*(2), 219–233.

Carless, D. (2013). Trust and its role in facilitating dialogic feedback. In D. Boud, & E. Molloy (Eds.), Feedback in higher and professional education: Understanding it and doing it well (pp. 90–103). London: Routledge.

Carless, D., & Boud, D. (2018). The development of student feedback literacy: Enabling uptake of feedback. *Assessment & Evaluation in Higher Education.* doi:10.1080/02602938.2018.1463354

Carless, D., Salter, D., Yang, M., & Lam, J. (2011). Developing sustainable feedback practices. *Studies in Higher Education, 36*(4), 395–407.

Cartney, P. (2010). Exploring the use of peer assessment as a vehicle for closing the gap between feedback given and feedback used. *Assessment & Evaluation in Higher Education, 35,* 551–564. doi:10.1080/02602931003632381

Castelijns, J. (2017). Op naar een feedbackcultuur. Leerbevorderende feedback binnen de context van High Impact Learning that lasts. Eindrapportage afstudeerproject LEH8.

Chanock, K. (2000). Comments on essays: Do students understand what tutors write? *Teaching in Higher Education, 5*(1), 95–105.

Chen, Z., Lam, W., & Zhong, J. A. (2007). Leader-member exchange and member performance: A new look at individual-level negative feedback-seeking behavior and team-level empowerment climate. *Journal of Applied Psychology, 92*(1), 202.

Cohen, J. (1988). Statistical power analysis for the behavioral sciences (2nd edn.). Hillsdale, NJ: Lawrence Erlbaum Associates.

Cotten, C., & Thompson, C. (2017). High-impact practices in social work education: A short-term study-abroad service-learning trip to Guatemala. *Journal of Social Work Education, 53*(4), 622–636.

Dawson, P., Henderson, M., Mahoney, P., Phillips, M., Ryan, T., Boud, D., & Molloy, E. (2019). What makes for effective feedback: Staff and student perspectives. *Assessment & Evaluation in Higher Education, 44*(1), 25–36.

Dempster, F. N. (1991). Synthesis of research on reviews and tests. *Educational Leadership, 48,* 71–76.

Dempster, F. N. (1992). Using tests to promote learning: A neglected classroom resource. *Journal of Research and Development in Education, 25,* 213–217.

DeNisi, A., & Sockbeson, C. E. S. (2018). Feedback sought vs feedback given: a tale of two literatures. *Management Research: Journal of the Iberoamerican Academy of Management*, 16(4), 320 -333. https://doi.org/10.1108/MRJIAM-09-2017-0778

DeNisi, A. S., Cafferty, T. P., & Meglino, B. M. (1984). A cognitive view of the performance appraisal process: A model and research propositions. *Organizational Behavior and Human Performance*, 33(3), 360–396.

De Stobbeleir, K. E., Ashford, S. J., & de Luque, M. F. S. (2010). Proactivity with image in mind: How employee and manager characteristics affect evaluations of proactive behaviours. *Journal of Occupational and Organizational Psychology*, 83(2), 347–369.

Dochy, F. (2005). 'Learning lasting for life' and 'assessment': How far did we progress? In Presidential address at the 20th anniversary of the European Association for Research on Learning and Instruction, Nicosia, Cyprus, August 23.

Dochy, Engeström, Sannino & Van Meeuwen (2021). Interorganisational expansive learning at work. In: F. Dochy, M. Segers, D. Gijbels, & P. Van den Bossche (Eds.), Theories of Workplace Learning in Changing Times. London/New York: Routledge.

Dochy, F., & Nickmans, G. (2005). Competentiegericht opleiden en toetsen: theorie en praktijk van flexibel leren. Utrecht: Lemma.

Dochy, F., & Segers, M. (2018). Creating impact through future learning: The high impact learning that lasts (HILL) model. London: Routledge.

Dochy, F., Segers, M., & Cascallar, E. (2003). Optimising new modes of assessment: In search of qualities and standards. Dordrecht: Springer Publishers.

Dochy, F., Dochy, W., & Janssens, M. (2018). Assessment-as-learning: De volgende stap in de toetsrevolutie. In D. Sluijsmans, & M. Segers (Eds.), Toetsrevolutie, Naar Een Feedbackcultuur in Het Hoger Onderwijs (pp. 23–34). Culemborg, NL: Uitgeverij Phronese.

Dochy, F., Segers, M., & Messmann, G. (2018). Informal learning at work: Triggers, antecendents and consequences. London: Taylor and Francis.

Dochy, F., Segers, M., & Sluijsmans, D. (1999). The use of self-, peer- and co-assessment in higher education. A review. *Studies in Higher Education*, 24, 331–350. doi:10.1080/03075079912331379935

Dochy, F., Segers, M., & Dochy, W. (2020). Bouwstenen voor high impact learning: Van model naar praktische tips en succescriteria. Amsterdam: Boom.

Dochy, F., Gijbels, D., Segers, M., & Van den Bossche, P. (2022). Theories of workplace learning in changing times. London/New York: Routledge.

Double, K. S., McGrane, J. A., & Hopfenbeck, T. N. (2020). The impact of peer assessment on academic performance: A meta-analysis of control group studies. *Educational Psychology Review* 32, 481–509. doi:10.1007/s10648-019-09510-3

Downes, S. (2005). An introduction to connective knowledge. http://www.downes.ca/cgi-bin/page.cgi?post=33034

Dowden, T., Pittaway, S., Yost, H., & McCarthy, R. (2013). Students' perceptions of written feedback in teacher education: Ideally feedback is a continuing two-way communication that encourages progress. *Assessment & Evaluation in Higher Education*, 38(3), 349–362.

Duijnhouwer, H. (2010). Feedback effects on students' writing motivation, process and performance. Doctoral dissertation. Utrecht University, the Netherlands.

Ecclestone, K. (1999). Empowering or ensnaring?: The implications of outcome-based assessment in higher education. *Higher Education Quarterly*, 53(1), 29–48. doi:10.1111/1468-2273.00111

Einbinder, S. D. (2018). A process and outcome evaluation of a one-semester faculty learning community: How universities can help faculty implement high impact practices. *InSight: A Journal of Scholarly Teaching*, 13, 40–58.

Elshout-Mohr, M. (1994). Feedback in self-instruction. *European Education*, 26(2), 58–73.

Esterhazy, R., & Damsa, C. (2017). Unpacking the feedback process: An analysis of undergraduate students' interactional meaning-making of feedback comments. *Studies in Higher Education*. doi:10.1080/03075079.2017.1359249

Evans, C. (2013). Making sense of assessment feedback in higher education. *Review of Educational Research*, 83(1), 70–120.

Falchikov, N. (2007). The place of peers in learning and assessment. In D. Boud, & N. Falchikov (Eds.), Rethinking assessment for higher education: Learning for the longer term (pp. 128–143). London: Routledge.

Falchikov, N., & Goldfinch, J. (2000). Student peer assessment in higher education: A meta-analysis comparing peer and teacher marks. *Review of Educational Research*, 70, 287–322.

Fedor, D. B. (1991). Recipient responses to performance feedback: A proposed model and its implications. In G. R. Ferris, & K. M. Rowland (Eds.), Research in personnel and human resource management (Vol. 9, pp. 73–120). Greenwich, CT: JAI Press.

Fedor, D. B., Eder, R. W., & Buckley, M. R. (1989). The contributory effects of supervisor intentions on subordinate feedback responses. *Organizational Behavior and Human Decision Processes*, 44(3), 396–414.

Ferguson, P. (2011). Student perceptions of quality feedback in teacher education. *Assessment & Evaluation in Higher Education*, 36, 51–62. doi:10.1080/02602930903197883

Ferris, G. R., Liden, R. C., Munyon, T. P., Summers, J. K., Basik, K. J., & Buckley, M. R. (2009). Relationships at work: Toward a multidimensional conceptualization of dyadic work relationships. *Journal of Management*, 35(6), 1379–1403.

Fisher, R., Cavanagh, J., & Bowles, A. (2011). Assisting transition to university: Using assessment as a formative learning tool. *Assessment and Evaluation in Higher Education*, 36, 225–237. doi:10.1080/02602930903308241

Fluckiger, J., Vigil, Y., Tixier, Y., Pasco, R., & Danielson, K. (2010). Formative feedback: Involving students as partners in assessment to enhance learning. *College Teaching*, 58, 136–140. doi:10.1080/87567555.2010.484031

Fredrickson, B. L. (2001). The role of positive emotions in positive psychology: The broaden-and-build theory of positive emotions. *American Psychologist*, 56(3), 218.

Fritz, C. O., & Morris, P. E. (2000). When further learning fails: Stability and change following repeated presentation of text. *British Journal of Psychology*, 91, 493–511. doi:10.1348/000712600161952

Gabelica, C., & Popov, V. (2020). 'One size does not fit all': Revisiting team feedback theories from a cultural dimensions perspective. *Group & Organization Management*, 45(2), 252–309. https://doi.org/10.1177/1059601120910859

Gabelica, C., Van den Bossche, P., Segers, M., & Gijselaers, W. (2012). Feedback, a powerful lever in teams: A review. *Educational Research Review*, 7(2), 123–144.

Gagné, M., & Deci, E. L. (2005). Self-determination theory and work motivation. *Journal of Organizational Behavior*, 26(4), 331–362.

Gibbs, G., & Simpson, C. (2004). Conditions under which assessment supports students' learning. *Learning and Teaching in Higher Education*, 1, 3–31.

Gielen, S., Dochy, F., & Dierick, S. (2003). Evaluating the consequential validity of new modes of assessment: The influence of assessment on learning, including pre-, post-, and true assessment effects. In M. Segers, F. Dochy, & E. Cascallar (Eds.), Optimising new modes of assessment: In search of qualities and standards (pp. 37–54). Dordrecht: Springer Netherlands.

Gielen, S., Dochy, F., & Onghena, P. (2011). An inventory of peer assessment diversity. *Assessment & Evaluation in Higher Education*, 36, 137–155. doi:10.1080/02602930903221444

Gielen, S., Peeters, E., Dochy, F., Onghena, P., & Struyven, K. (2010). Improving the effectiveness of peer feedback for learning. *Learning and Instruction*, 20, 304–315. doi:10.1016/j.learninstruc.2009.08.007

Gielen, S., Tops, L., Dochy, F., Onghena, P., & Smeets, S. (2010). A comparative study of peer and teacher feedback and of various peer feedback forms in a secondary school writing curriculum. *British Educational Research Journal*, 36(1), 143–162.

Gielen, S., Dochy, F., Onghena, P., Struyven, K., & Smeets, S. (2011). Goals of peer assessment and their associated quality concepts. *Studies in Higher Education*, 36, 719–735. doi:10.1080/03075071003759037

Gilbert, L., Whitelock, D., & Gale, V. (2011). Synthesis report on assessment and feedback with technology enhancement. Southampton, UK: Electronics and Computer Science EPrints.

Graen, G. B., & Scandura, T. A. (1987). Toward a psychology of dyadic organizing. *Research in Organizational Behavior*, 9, 175–208.

Graen, G. B., & Uhl-Bien, M. (1995). Relationship-based approach to leadership: Development of leader-member exchange (LMX) theory of leadership over 25 years: Applying a multi-level multi-domain perspective. *The Leadership Quarterly*, 6(2), 219–247.

Graziano-King, J. (2007). Assessing student writing: The self-revised essay. *Journal of Basic Writing (CUNY)*, 26, 75–94.

Goulette, N., & Denney, A. S. (2018). Probation simulation: A high-impact practice. *Journal of Criminal Justice Education*, 29(3), 370–398.

Handley, K., & Cox, B. (2007). Beyond model answers: Learners' perceptions of self-assessment materials in e-learning applications. *ALT-J Research in Learning Technology*, 15, 21–36. doi:10.1080/09687760601129539

Handley, K., Price, M., & Millar, J. (2008). Engaging students with assessment feedback. Final report for FDTL project 144/03. Retrieved from http://www. brookes. ac.uk/aske/documents/FDTL_FeedbackProjectReportApril2009.pdf

Harrison, S. H., & Rouse, E. D. (2015). An inductive study of feedback interactions over the course of creative projects. *Academy of Management Journal*, 58(2), 375–404.

Harland, T., & Wald, N. (2021). The assessment arms race and the evolution of a university's assessment practices. *Assessment & Evaluation in Higher Education*, 46(1), 105–117. doi:10.1080/02602938.2020.1745753

Harlen, W. & Deakin Crick, R. (2003). Testing and motivation for learning. *Assessment in Education*, 10(2), 169–207.

Hattie, J. (2012). Visible learning for teachers: Maximizing impact on learning. London: Routledge.

Hattie, J., & Timperley, H. (2007). The power of feedback. *Review of Educational Research*, 77(1), 81–112. doi:10.3102/003465430298487

Hays, J. C., & Williams, J. R. (2011). Testing multiple motives in feedback seeking: The interaction of instrumentality and self-protection motives. *Journal of Vocational Behavior*, 79(2), 496–504.

Higgins, R., Hartley, P., & Skelton, A. (2001). Getting the message across: The problem of communicating assessment feedback. *Teaching in Higher Education*, 6, 269–274. doi:10.1080/13562510120045230

Hill, J., & West, H. (2020). Improving the student learning experience through dialogic feed-forward assessment. *Assessment & Evaluation in Higher Education*, 45(1), 82–97. doi:10.1080/02602938.2019.1608908

Huisman, B., Saab, N., van den Broek, P., & van Driel, J. (2019). The impact of formative peer feedback on higher education students' academic writing: A meta-analysis. *Assessment & Evaluation in Higher Education*, 44(6), 863–880.

Huxham, M. (2007). Fast and effective feedback: Are model answers the answer? *Assessment and Evaluation in Higher Education*, 32, 601–611. doi:10.1080/02602930601116946

Ilgen, D. R. (1971). Satisfaction with performance as a function of the initial level of expected performance and the deviation from expectations. *Organizational Behavior and Human Performance*, 6(3), 345–361.

Ilgen, D. R., & Hamstra, B. W. (1972). Performance satisfaction as a function of the difference between expected and reported performance at five levels of reported performance. *Organizational Behavior and Human Performance*, 7(3), 359–370.

Ilgen, D. R., Fisher, C. D., & Taylor, M. S. (1979). Consequences of individual feedback on behavior in organizations. *Journal of Applied Psychology*, 64(4), 349–371.

Ilies, R., De Pater, I. E., & Judge, T. (2007). Differential affective reactions to negative and positive feedback, and the role of self-esteem. *Journal of Managerial Psychology*, 22(6), 590–609.

Isaacs, W. (1994). Team learning. In P. Senge, A. Kleiner, C. Roberts, R. B. Ross, & B. J. Smith (Eds.), The fifth discipline fieldbook: Strategies and tools for building a learning organization (pp. 357–444). New York, NY: Doubleday.

Ishaq, F. J., & Bass, J. (2019). High impact educational practices and the student athlete experience: The implementation and barriers of HIPs in the student athlete support setting. *Journal of Issues in Intercollegiate Athletics*, 12, 178–204.

Ivanic, R., Clark, R., & Rimmershaw, R. (2000). What am I supposed to make of this?: The messages conveyed to students by tutors' written comments. In M. Lea, & B. Stierer (Eds.), Student writing in higher education: New contexts (pp. 47–65). Buckingham: Open University Press.

Jabri, M. (2004). Team feedback based on dialogue: Implications for change management. *Journal of Management Development*, 23(2), 141–151. https://doi-org.mu.idm.oclc.org/10.1108/02621710410517238

James, M. (2006). Assessment, teaching and theories of learning. In J. Gardner (Ed.), Assessment and learning (pp. 47–60). London: Sage.

James, M. (2012). Chapter 12: Assessment in harmony with our understanding of learning: Problems and possibilities. In J. Gardner (Ed.), Assessment and learning (2nd edn.) (pp. 187–205). London: Sage.

Jawahar, I. M. (2010). The mediating role of appraisal feedback reactions on the relationship between rater feedback-related behaviors and ratee performance. *Group & Organization Management*, 35(4), 494–526.

Jonsson, A. (2013). Facilitating productive use of feedback in higher education. *Active Learning in Higher Education*, 14(1), 63–76.

Jonsson, A., Mattheos, N., Svingby, G., & Attström, R. (2007). Dynamic assessment and the 'Interactive examination'. *Journal of Educational Technology & Society*, 10(4), 17–27.

Kahmann, K. (2009). *Die Erfassung der Feedbackkultur in Organisationen. Die Erfassung und psychometrische Überprüfung eines Messinstruments*. PhD thesis. Hamburg: Verlag Dr. Kovac.

Kinicki, A. J., Prussia, G. E., Wu, B. J., & McKee-Ryan, F. M. (2004). A covariance structure analysis of employees' response to performance feedback. *Journal of Applied Psychology*, 89(6), 1057.

Klich, N. R., & Feldman, D. C. (1992). The role of approval and achievement needs in feedback seeking behavior. *Journal of Managerial Issues*, 4(4), 554–570.

Kluger, A. N., & DeNisi, A. (1996). The effects of feedback interventions on performance: A historical review, a meta-analysis, and a preliminary feedback intervention theory. *Psychological Bulletin*, 119, 254–284. doi:10.1037/00332909.119.2.254

Knight, J. (2009). Coaching. *Journal of Staff Development*, 30(1), 18–22.

Kori, K., Pedaste, M., Leijen, Ä, & Mäeots, M. (2014). Supporting reflection in technology-enhanced learning. *Educational Research Review*, 11, 45–55.

Korthagen, F., & Nuijten, E. (2020). Krachtgericht coachen. Amsterdam: Boom.

Kram, K. E., & Isabella, L. A. (1985). Mentoring alternatives: The role of peer relationships in career development. *Academy of Management Journal*, 28(1), 110–132.

Kulhavy, R. W. (1977). Feedback in written instruction. *Review of Educational Research*, 47, 211–232.

Lam, W., Huang, X., & Snape, E. D. (2007). Feedback-seeking behavior and leader-member exchange: Do supervisor-attributed motives matter? *Academy of Management Journal*, 50(2), 348–363.

Larson, J. R., Jr. (1984). The performance feedback process: A preliminary model. *Organizational Behavior and Human Performance*, 33(1), 42–76.

Larson, J. R., Jr, Glynn, M. A., Fleenor, C. P., & Scontrino, M. P. (1986). Exploring the dimensionality of managers' performance feedback to subordinates. *Human Relations*, 39(12), 1083–1101.

Lee, I. (2008). Student reactions to teacher feedback in two Hong Kong secondary classrooms. *Journal of Second Language Writing*, 17, 144–164.

Lipnevich, A. A., & Smith, J. K. (2009). Effects of differential feedback on students' examination performance. *Journal of Experimental Psychology: Applied*, 15(4), 319.

Lipnevich, A. A., Berg, D. A. G., & Smith, J. K. (2016). Toward a model of student response to feedback. In G. T. L. Brown, & L. R. Harris (Eds.), Handbook of human and social conditions in assessment (pp. 169–185). New York: Routledge.

Liu, N. F., & Carless, D. (2006). Peer feedback: The learning element of peer assessment. *Teaching in Higher Education*, 11, 279–290.

London, M. (2003). Job feedback: Giving, seeking, and using feedback for performance improvement. Mahwah (NJ)/London: Lawrence Erlbaum Associates, Publishers.

London, M., & Sessa, V. I. (2006). Group feedback for continuous learning. *Human Resource Development Review*, 5(3), 303–329.

Losada, M., & Heaphy, E. (2004). The role of positivity and connectivity in the performance of business teams: A nonlinear dynamics model. *American Behavioral Scientist*, 47, 740–765.

Maclellan, E. (2001). Assessment for learning: The differing perceptions of tutors and students. *Assessment & Evaluation in Higher Education*, 26(4), 307–318.

Martens, R., & Dochy, F. (1997). Assessment and feedback as student support devices. *Studies in Educational Evaluation*, 23, 257–273.

McDowell, L. (2008). Students' experiences of feedback on academic assignments in higher education: implications for practice. In A. Haves, & L. McDowell (Eds.), Balancing dilemmas in assessment and learning in contemporary education (pp. 237–249). London: Routledge.

Miller, C., Doering, A., & Scharber, C. (2010). No such thing as failure, only feedback: Designing innovative opportunities for e-assessment and technology-mediated feedback. *Journal of Interactive Learning Research*, 21, 197–224.

Miller, R. L., Rycek, R. F., & Fritson, K. (2011). The effects of high impact learning experiences on student engagement. *Procedia – Social and Behavioral Sciences*, 15, 53–59.

Moerkerke, G. (1996). Assessment for flexible learning. Heerlen: Open University.

Morran, D. K., Robison, F. F., & Stockton, R. (1985). Feedback exchange in counseling groups: An analysis of message content and receiver acceptance as a function of leader versus member delivery, session, and valence. *Journal of Counseling Psychology*, 32(1), 57.

Morrison, E. W., & Bies, R. J. (1991). Impression management in the feedback-seeking process: A literature review and research agenda. *Academy of Management Review*, 16(3), 522–541.

Morrison, E. W., & Vancouver, J. B. (2000). Within-person analysis of information seeking: The effects of perceived costs and benefits. *Journal of Management*, 26(1), 119–137.

Moss, S. E., Sanchez, J. I., Brumbaugh, A. M., & Borkowski, N. (2009). The mediating role of feedback avoidance behavior in the LMX – Performance relationship. *Group & Organization Management*, 34(6), 645–664.

Mulder, R. H., & Ellinger, A. D. (2013). Exploring feedback incidents, their characteristics and the informal learning activities that emanate from them. *European Journal of Training and Development*, 37(1), 49–71.

Murphrey, T. P., Odom, S. F., & Sledd, J. (2016). An examination of university agricultural education faculty attitudes toward the implementation of high impact learning experiences. *Journal of Agricultural Education*, 57(3), 162–179.

Myers, C. B., Myers, S. M., & Peters, M. (2019). The longitudinal connections between undergraduate high impact curriculum practices and civic engagement in adulthood. *Research in Higher Education*, 60(1), 83–110.

Nakai, Y., & O'Malley, A. L. (2015). Feedback to know, to show, or both? A profile approach to the feedback process. *Learning and Individual Differences*, 43, 1–10.

Nicol, D. (2009). Assessment for learner self-regulation: Enhancing achievement in the first year using learner technologies. *Assessment & Evaluation in Higher Education*, 34(3), 335–352.

Nicol, D. (2010). From monologue to dialogue: Improving written feedback processes in mass higher education. *Assessment & Evaluation in Higher Education*, 35(5), 501–517.

Nicol, D. J., & MacFarlane-Dick, D. (2006). Formative assessment and self-regulated learning: A model and seven principles of good feedback practice. *Studies in Higher Education*, 31, 199–218. doi:10.1080/03075070600572090

Northcraft, G. B., & Ashford, S. J. (1990). The preservation of self in everyday life: The effects of performance expectations and feedback context on feedback inquiry. *Organizational Behavior and Human Decision Processes*, 47(1), 42–64.

O'Donovan, B., Rust, C., & Price, M. (2016). A scholarly approach to solving the feedback dilemma in practice. *Assessment & Evaluation in Higher Education*, 41(6), 938–949.

Panadero, E. (2016). Is it safe? Social, interpersonal, and human effects of peer assessment: a review and future directions. In G. T. L. Brown, & L. R. Harris (Eds.), Handbook of human and social conditions in assessment (pp. 247–266). New York: Routledge.

Panadero, E., & Jonsson, A. (2013). The use of scoring rubrics for formative assessment purposes revisited: A review. *Educational Research Review*, 9, 129–144.

Panadero, E., & Jonsson, A. (2020). A critical review of the arguments against the use of rubrics. *Educational Research Review*, 30, 300–329.

Panadero, E., Jonsson, A., & Botella, J. (2017). Effects of self-assessment on self-regulated learning and self-efficacy: Four meta-analyses. *Educational Research Review*, 22, 74–98. doi:10.1016/j.edurev.2017.08.004

Panadero, E., Jonsson, A., & Alqassab, M. (2018). Peer feedback used for formative purposes: review of findings. In A. Lipnevich & J. K. Smith (Eds.), The Cambridge handbook of instructional feedback. Cambridge, UK: Cambridge University Press.

Panadero, E., Lipnevich, A., & Broadbent, J. (2019). Turning self-assessment into self-feedback. The impact of feedback in higher education (pp. 147–163). Cham: Palgrave Macmillan.

Papinczak, T., Young, L., & Groves, M. (2007). Peer assessment in problem-based learning: A qualitative study. *Advances in Health Sciences Education*, 12, 169–186. doi:10.1007/s10459-005-5046-6

Pardo, A., Jovanovic, J., Dawson, S., Gašević, D., & Mirriahi, N. (2017). Using learning analytics to scale the provision of personalized feedback. *British Journal of Educational Technology*. doi:10.1111/bjet.12592

Parker, P. M., & Baughan, P. (2011). Providing written feedback that students will value and read. *The International Journal of Learning*, 16(11), 253–262.

Parkes, M., & Fletcher, M. (2017). A longitudinal, quantitative study of student attitudes towards audio feedback for assessment. *Assessment & Evaluation in Higher Education*, 42(7), 1046–1053.

Pintrich, P. R., & Zusho, A. (2002). Student motivation and self-regulated learning in the college classroom, In J. C. Smart, & W. G. Tierney (Eds.), Higher education: Handbook of theory and research (vol. XVII). New York: Agathon Press.

Poulos, A., & Mahony, M. J. (2008). Effectiveness of feedback: The students' perspective. *Assessment and Evaluation in Higher Education, 33*, 143–154. doi:10.1080/02602930601127869

Price, M., Handley, K., & Millar, J. (2011). Feedback: Focusing attention on engagement. *Studies in Higher Education, 36*(8), 879–896. doi:10.1080/03075079.2010.483513

Reid, D. H., & Parsons, M. B. (1996). A comparison of staff acceptability of immediate versus delayed verbal feedback in staff training. *Journal of Organizational Behavior Management, 16*(2), 35–47.

Semler, R. (1993). Maverick: The success story behind the world's most unusual work. New York, NY: Warner Books.

Semler, R. (2003). The seven-day weekend: Finding the work/life balance. London: Century.

Sendzuik, P. (2010). Sink or swim? Improving student learning through feedback and self-assessment. *International Journal of Teaching and Learning in Higher Education, 22*(30), 320–330.

Shrauger, J. S., & Rosenberg, S. E. (1970). Self-esteem and the effects of success and failure feedback on performance 1. *Journal of Personality, 38*(3), 404–417.

Siemens, G. (2005). Connectivism: A learning theory for the digital age. *International Journal of Instructional Technology and Distance Learning, 2*, 1. http://www.itdl.org/Journal/Jan_05/article01.htm

Shute, V. J. (2008). Focus on formative feedback. *Review of Educational Research, 78*, 153–189. doi:10.3102/0034654307313795

Sias, P. M. (2015). Workplace friendships. *The International Encyclopedia of Interpersonal Communication, 1*, 1–5.

Sias, P. M., Krone, K. J., & Jablin, F. M. (2002). An ecological systems perspective on workplace relationships. *Handbook of Interpersonal Communication, 3*, 615–642.

Smith, C. (2021). How does the medium affect the message? Architecture students' perceptions of the relative utility of different feedback methods. *Assessment & Evaluation in Higher Education, 46*(1), 54–67. doi:10.1080/02602938.2020.1733489

Soderström, N. C., & Bjork, R. A. (2015). Learning versus performance: An integrative review. *Perspectives on Psychological Science, 10*, 176–199.

Steelman, L. A., & Rutkowski, K. A. (2004). Moderators of employee reactions to negative feedback. *Journal of Managerial Psychology, 19*(1), 6–18.

Steen-Utheim, A., & Wittek, A. (2017). Dialogic feedback and potentialities for student learning. *Learning, Culture and Social Interaction, 15*, 18–30.

Sutcliffe, R., Linfield, R., Riley, G., Nabb, D., & Glazzard, J. (2019). The search for 100% satisfaction with feedback. *Teacher Education Advancement Network Journal, 11*(3), 35–47.

Sutton, P. (2012). Conceptualizing feedback literacy: Knowing, being, and acting. *Innovations in Education and Teaching International, 49*(1), 31–40.

Taras, M. (2003). To feedback or not to feedback in student self-assessment. *Assessment and Evaluation in Higher Education*, 28, 549–565. doi:10.1080/02602930301678

Taras, M. (2006). Do unto others or not: Equity in feedback for undergraduates. *Assessment & Evaluation in Higher Education*, 31(3), 365–377.

Thurlings, M., Vermeulen, M., Bastiaens, T., & Stijnen, S. (2013). Understanding feedback: A learning theory perspective. *Educational Research Review*, 9, 1–15.

Topping, K. J. (1998). Peer assessment between students in colleges and universities. *Review of Educational Research*, 68, 249–276.

Topping, K. J. (2010). Methodological quandaries in studying process and outcomes in peer assessment. *Learning and Instruction*, 20, 339–343. doi:10.1016/j.learninstruc.2009.08.003

Tuckey, M., Brewer, N., & Williamson, P. (2002). The influence of motives and goal orientation on feedback seeking. *Journal of Occupational and Organizational Psychology*, 75(2), 195–216.

Tuckey, M., Brewer, N., & Barnes, K. (2006). Source attributes and feedback seeking: a field study. *International Journal of Organisational Behaviour*, 11(1), 20-30.

Van Dinther, M., Dochy, F., & Segers, M. (2011). Factors affecting students' self-efficacy in higher education. *Educational Research Review*, 6(2), 95–108.

van Gennip, N., Segers, M., & Tillema, H. H. (2009). Peer assessment for learning from a social perspective: The influence of interpersonal variables and structural features. *Educational Research Review*, 4, 41–54. doi:10.1016/j.edurev.2008.11.002

van Gennip, N., Segers, M., & Tillema, H. H. (2010). Peer assessment as a collaborative learning activity: The role of interpersonal variables and conceptions. *Learning and Instruction*, 20, 280–290. doi:10.1016/j.learninstruc.2009.08.010

Vancouver, J. B., & Morrison, E. W. (1995). Feedback inquiry: The effect of source attributes and individual differences. *Organizational Behavior and Human Decision Processes*, 62(3), 276–285.

VandeWalle, D. (2003). A goal orientation model of feedback-seeking behavior. *Human Resource Management Review*, 13(4), 581–604.

Värlander, S. (2008). The role of students' emotions in formal feedback situations. *Teaching in Higher Education*, 13(2), 145–156.

Vedder, P. (1985). Cooperative learning: A study on processes and effects of cooperation between primary school children. Groningen, the Netherlands: Rijkuniversiteit Groningen.

Voerman, L., & Faber, F. (2010). 'Goed zo!' Is onvoldoende. *Van 12 Tot*, 18(6), 48–49.

Voerman, L., Meijer, P. C., Korthagen, F. A., & Simons, R. J. (2012). Types and frequencies of feedback interventions in classroom interaction in secondary education. *Teaching and Teacher Education*, 28(8), 1107–1115.

Voerman, L., Meijer, P. C., Korthagen, F. A. J., & Simons, P. R. J. (2014). Feedback revisited: Adding perspectives based on positive psychology. Implications for theory and classroom practice. *Teaching and Teacher Education*, 43, 41–98.

Walker, M. (2009). An investigation into written comments on assignments: Do students find them usable? *Assessment and Evaluation in Higher Education*, 34, 67–78. doi:10.1080/02602930801895752

Wang, M., Burlacu, G., Truxillo, D., James, K., & Yao, X. (2015). Age differences in feedback reactions: The roles of employee feedback orientation on social awareness and utility. *Journal of Applied Psychology*, 100(4), 1296.

Wass, R., Harland, T., McLean, A., Miller, E., & Sim, K. N. (2015). 'Will press lever for food': Behavioural conditioning of students through frequent high-stakes assessment. *Higher Education Research & Development*, 34(6), 1324–1326.

Weaver, M. R. (2006). Do students value feedback? Student perceptions of tutors' written responses. *Assessment and Evaluation in Higher Education*, 31, 379–394. doi:10.1080/02602930500353061

Weber, K., & Myrick, K. (2018). Reflecting on reflecting: Summer undergraduate research Students' experiences in developing electronic portfolios, a meta-high impact practice. *International Journal of ePortfolio*, 8(1), 13–25.

Wenger, E., McDermott, R., & Synder, W. M. (2002). Cultivating communities of practice. Boston, MA: Harvard Business School Press.

Wiliam, D. (2011). What is assessment for learning? *Studies in Educational Evaluation*, 37, 3–14. doi:10.1016/j.stueduc.2011.03.001

Wiliam, D. (2018). Feedback: at the heart of-but definitely not all of-formative assessment. The Cambridge handbook of instructional feedback (pp. 3–28). Cambridge, UK: Cambridge University Press.

Wingate, U. (2010). The impact of formative feedback on the development of academic writing. *Assessment and Evaluation in Higher Education*, 35, 519–533. doi:10.1080/02602930903512909

Winstone, N., & Carless, D. (2019). Designing effective feedback processes in higher education: A learning-focused approach. London: Routledge.

Winstone, N. E., Nash, R. A., Parker, M., & Rowntree, J. (2017). Supporting Learners' agentic engagement with feedback: A systematic review and a taxonomy of recipience processes, *Educational Psychologist*, 52(1), 17–37. doi:10.1080/00461520.2016.1207538

Wisniewski, B., Zierer, K., & Hattie, J. (2020). The power of feedback revisited: A meta-analysis of educational feedback research. *Frontiers in Psychology*, 10, 3087.

Wu, Y., & Schunn, C. D. (2020). When peers agree, do students listen? The central role of feedback quality and feedback frequency in determining uptake of feedback. *Contemporary Educational Psychology*, 62, 101897.

Xiao, Y., & Lucking, R. (2008). The impact of two types of peer assessment on students' performance and satisfaction within a wiki environment. *Internet and Higher Education*, 11, 186–193. doi:10.1016/j.iheduc.2008.06.005

Yang, M., & Carless, D. (2013). The feedback triangle and the enhancement of dialogic feedback processes. *Teaching in Higher Education*, 18(3), 285–297.

Yang, M., Badger, R., & Yu, Z. (2006). A comparative study of peer and teacher feedback in a Chinese EFL writing class. *Journal of Second Language Writing*, 15, 179–200.

Young, P. (2000). 'I might as well give up': Self-esteem and mature students' feelings about feedback on assignments. *Journal of Further and Higher Education*, 24, 409–418. doi:10.1080/030987700750022325

Zhao, H. (2010). Investigating learners' use and understanding of peer and teacher feedback on writing: A comparative study in a Chinese English writing class-room. *Assessing Writing*, 15(1), 3–17.

Zhou, J. (1998). Feedback valence, feedback style, task autonomy, and achievement orientation: Interactive effects on creative performance. *Journal of Applied Psychology*, 83(2), 261.

Zhou, J., Dawson, P., Tai, J., & Bearman, M. (2021). How conceptualising respect can inform feedback pedagogies. *Assessment & Evaluation in Higher Education*, 46(1), 68–79. doi:10.1080/02602938.2020.1733490

Zilvinskis, J., & Dumford, A. D. (2018). The relationship between transfer student status, student engagement, and high-impact practice participation. *Community College Review*, 46(4), 368–387.

For Product Safety Concerns and Information please contact our EU
representative GPSR@taylorandfrancis.com
Taylor & Francis Verlag GmbH, Kaufingerstraße 24, 80331 München, Germany

9 7 8 1 0 3 2 2 7 7 9 8 1